Horace Walpole, Paul Hentzner, Richard Bentley

Paul Hentzner's Travels in England

During the Reign of Queen Elizabeth

Horace Walpole, Paul Hentzner, Richard Bentley

Paul Hentzner's Travels in England
During the Reign of Queen Elizabeth

ISBN/EAN: 9783337345952

Printed in Europe, USA, Canada, Australia, Japan

Cover: Foto ©Thomas Meinert / pixelio.de

More available books at **www.hansebooks.com**

Queen Elizabeth.

From an Original Drawing by Zuccaro done by order of the Parliament

Pub.d Jan.y 1 1797 by E Jefferys

PAUL HENTZNER's
TRAVELS
IN
ENGLAND,

During the Reign of QUEEN ELIZABETH,

TRANSLATED BY

HORACE, LATE EARL OF ORFORD,

AND FIRST PRINTED BY HIM AT

STRAWBERRY HILL:

TO WHICH IS NOW ADDED,

SIR ROBERT NAUNTON's
FRAGMENTA REGALIA;

OR,

OBSERVATIONS ON QUEEN ELIZABETH'S

TIMES AND FAVOURITES;

WITH

PORTRAITS AND VIEWS.

London:

Printed for EDWARD JEFFERY, oppofite
Carlton Houfe, Pall-Mall.

1797.

Price 15s. in Boards; and 1l. 1s. bound in Morocco.

TO THE

RIGHT HONOURABLE

HUGH,

LORD *WILLOUGHBY* of *PARHAM*,

PRESIDENT;

TO THE

COUNCIL AND FELLOWS

OF THE

Society of Antiquaries,

This EDITION and TRANSLATION of Part of the ITINERARY of

HENTZNERUS,

Is offered with great Respect

by the EDITOR,

HORACE WALPOLE, F. S. A., and F. R. S.

ADVERTISEMENT.

Doctor Birch, in his Summary of Sir Thomas Edmondes's State-papers, has published a short extract from the following obsolete author, which, for the elegance of the Latin, and the remarkable description of queen Elizabeth, has been deservedly admired: her best portraits scarcely exhibit a more lively image.

The original work, of which, perhaps, there are not above four or five copies in England, is an Itinerary through Germany, England, France, and Italy, performed by Hentzner, a travelling tutor to a young German nobleman. That Dr. Birch has extracted the most interesting passage in the whole book is certain: yet it records some circumstances and customs not unworthy the notice of an English antiquarian, and which are mentioned no where else. For these reasons, I flatter myself, that a publication of the part relating to our own country might not be an unacceptable present to persons of curiosity.

The tranflation was the production of the idle hours of another gentleman.

The author feems to have had that laborious and indifcriminate paffion for SEEING which is remarked in his countrymen; and, as his tranflator obferved, enjoyed as much the doubtful head, of a more doubtful faint in pickle, as any upon the fhoulders of the beft Grecian ftatue. Fortunately fo memorable a perfonage as queen Elizabeth, happened to fall under his notice!—Ten years later, he would have been as accurate in painting Anne of Denmark!

The excefs of refpectful ceremonial ufed at decking her majefty's table, though not in her prefence, and the kind of adoration and genuflection paid to her perfon, approach to Eaftern homage. When we obferve fuch worfhip offered to an old woman, with bare neck, black teeth, and falfe red hair, it makes one fmile; but makes one reflect what mafculine fenfe was couched under thofe weakneffes, and which could command fuch awe from a nation like England!

Not to anticipate the entertainment of the reader, I fhall make but one more reflection. We are apt to think that fir William Temple, and king William, were in a manner the introducers of gardening into England: by the defcription of lord Burleigh's gardens at Theobalds, and of thofe at Nonfuch, we find that the magnificent, though falfe, tafte, was known here as early as the reigns of Henry VIII. and his daughter. There is fcarce an unnatural and fumptuous impropriety at Verfailles, which we do not find in Hentzner's defcription of the gardens above mentioned.

With regard to the orthography of proper names, though correɕted in the tranflation, I have left them in the original as I found them——Accuracy in that particular, was not the author's merit: it is a merit peculiar to Englifhmen: the French are negligent of it to an affectation; yet the author of *Les Melanges Hiftoriques* complains that other nations corrupt French names! He himfelf gives fome Englifh ones in p. 247, 248, which it is impoffible to decypher. Baffompierre calls Yorkhoufe, *Jorchaux*, and Kenfington, *Inhimthort*. As a foldier and embaffador, he was not obliged to know the names of houses; when he turned author, there was no excuse for not being intelligible. Even Voltaire, who writes the language so well, is careless in our titles. In England, it is the defect of a servant to blunder in proper names. It is one of those silly pretensions to politeness, which nations that affect a superiority, have always cultivated----For in all affectations, defects are merits. The readers of history love certainty: it is pity the writers do not. What confusion would it have saved, if it had not been the custom of the Jews to call every Darius and Artaxerxes, Ahasuerus! It were to be wished, that all nations would be content to use the appellations which people, or respective countries have chosen for themselves. Proper names ought never to be tortured to any particular idiom. What a ridiculous composition is *Aulugel!* Who can conceive that *Meylandt,* signifies Milan; or Leghorn, *Livorno?* When one is misled by a proper name, the only use of which is to direct, one feels like the countryman, who complained, *That the houses hindered him from seeing Paris.*----The thing becomes an obstruction to itself.

HENTZNER'S

TRAVELS.

WE arrived at Rye, a small English sea-port. Here, as soon as we came on shore, we gave in our names to the notary of the place, but not till he had demanded our business; and being answered, that we had none but to see England, we were conducted to an inn, where we were very well entertained; as one generally is in this country.

We took post horses for London: it is surprising how swiftly they run; their bridles are very light, and their saddles little more than a span over.

Flimwell, a village: here we returned our first horses, and mounted fresh ones.

We passed through Tunbridge, another village.

Chepstead, another village: here, for the second time, we changed horses.

London, the head and metropolis of England: called by Tacitus, Londinium; by Ptolomy, Logidinium; by Ammianus Marcellinus, Lundinium; by foreigners, Londra, and Londres; it is the seat of the British empire, and the chamber of the English kings. This most ancient city is in the county of Middlesex, the fruitfullest and wholesomest soil in England. It is built on the river Thames, sixty miles from the sea, and was originally founded, as all historians agree, by Brutus, who coming from Greece into Italy, thence into Africa, next into France, and last into Britain, chose this situation for the convenience of the river, calling it Troja Nova, which name was afterwards corrupted into Trinovant. But when Lud, the brother of Cassibilan, or Cassivelan, who warred against Julius Cæsar, as he himself mentions, lib. v. de Bell. Gall. came to the crown, he encompassed it with very strong walls, and towers very artfully constructed, and from his own name called it Caier Lud. i. e. Lud's City. This name was corrupted into that of Caerlunda, and again in time by change of language, into Londres. Lud, when he died, was buried in this town, near that gate which is yet called in Welsh, Por Lud, in Saxon, Ludesgate.

The famous river Thames owes part of its stream, as well as its appellation, to the Isis; rising a little above Winchelcomb, and being increased with several rivulets, unites both its waters and its name to the Thame, on the other side of Oxford; thence, after passing by London, and being of the utmost utility, from its greatness and navigation, it opens into a vast arm of the sea, from whence the tide, according to Gemma Frisius, flows and ebbs to the distance of eighty miles, twice in twenty-five hours, and, according to Polydore Vergil, above sixty miles twice in twenty four hours.

This city being very large of itself, has very extensive suburbs, and a fort called the Tower, of beautiful structure. It is magnificently ornamented, with public buildings and churches, of which there are above one hundred and twenty parochial.

On the south, is a bridge of stone eight hundred feet in length, of wonderful work; it is supported upon twenty piers of square stone, sixty feet high, and thirty broad, joined by arches of about twenty feet diameter. The whole is covered on each side with houses, so disposed, as to have the appearance of a continued street, not at all of a bridge.

Upon this is built a tower, on whose top the heads of such as have been executed for high treason, are placed on iron spikes: we counted above thirty.

Paulus Jovius, in his description of the most remarkable towns in England, says, all are obscured by London: which in the opinion of many, is Cæsar's city of the Trinobantes, the capital of all Britain, famous for the commerce of many nations; its houses are elegantly built, its churches fine, its towns strong, and its riches and abundance surprising. The wealth of the world is wafted to it by the Thames, swelled by the tide, and navigable to merchant ships, through a safe and deep channel for sixty miles, from its mouth to the city: its banks are every were beautified with fine country seats, woods, and farms; below, is the royal palace of Greenwich; above, that of Richmond; and between both, on the west of London, rise the noble buildings of Westminster, most remarkable for the courts of justice, the parliament, and St. Peter's church, enriched with the royal tombs. At the distance of twenty miles from London, is the castle of Windsor, a most delightful retreat of the kings of England, as well as famous for several of their tombs, and for the ceremonial of the order of the Garter. This river abounds in swans, swimming in flocks: the sight of them and their noise, is vastly agreeable to the fleets that meet them in their course. It is joined to the city by a bridge of stone, wonderfully built; is never increased by any rains, rising only with the tide, and is every were spread with nets for taking salmon and shad. Thus far Paulus Jovius.

Polydore Vergil affirms, that London has continued to be a royal city, and the capital of the kingdom, crowded with its own inhabitants and foreigners, abounding in riches, and famous for its great trade, from the time of king Archeninus, or Erchenvinus. Here the kings are crowned; and folemnly inaugurated, and the council of the nation, or parliament, is held. The government of the city is lodged, by antient grant of the kings of Britain, in twenty-four aldermen, that is, feniors: thefe annually elect out of their own body a mayor, and two fheriffs, who determine caufes according to municipal laws. It has always had, as indeed Britain in general has, a great number of men of learning, much diftinguifhed for their writings.

The walls are pierced with fix gates, which, as they were rebuilt, acquired new names. Two look weftward:

1. Ludgate, the oldeft, fo called from king Lud, whofe name is yet to be feen, cut in the ftone over the arch on the fide; though others imagine it rather to have been named Fludgate, from a ftream over which it ftands, like the Porta Fluentana at Rome. It has been lately repaired by queen Elizabeth, whofe ftatue is placed on the oppofite fide. And,

2. Newgate, the beft edifice of any: fo called from being new built, whereas before it was named Chamberlain gate. It is the public prifon.

On the north are four:

1. Alderfgate, as fome think from alder trees; as others, from Aldericius, a Saxon.

2. Cripplegate, from an hospital for the lame.

3. Moorgate, from a neighbouring morass, now converted into a field, first opened by Francetius * the mayor, A. D. 1414.

4. And Bishopsgate, from some bishop: this the German merchants of the Hans society were obilged by compact to keep in repair, and in times of danger to defend. They were in possession of a key, to open or shut it, so that upon occasion they could come in, or go out, by night, or by day.

There is only one to the east:

Aldgate, that is, Oldgate, from its antiquity; though others think it to have been named Elbegate.

Several people believe, that there were formerly two gates (besides that to the bridge,) towards the Thames.

1. Billingsgate, now a cothon, or artificial port, for the reception of ships.

2. Dourgate, vulgo Dowgate, i. e. Water-gate.

The cathedral of St. Paul was founded by Ethelbert, king of the Saxons, and being from time to

* His name was Sir Thomas Falconer.

time re-edified, increased to vastness and magnificence, and in revenue so much, that it affords a plentiful support to a bishop, dean, and præcentor, treasurer, four archdeacons, twenty-nine prebendaries, and many others. The roof of this church, as of most others in England, with the adjoining steeple, is covered with lead.

On the right side of the choir is the marble tomb of Nicholas Bacon, with his wife. Not far from this is a magnificent monument, ornamented with pyramids of marble, and alabaster, with this inscription:

Sacred to the memory of

Sir Christopher Hatton, son of William, grandson of John, of the most antient family of the Hattons, one of the fifty gentlemen pensioners to her majesty queen Elizabeth: Gentleman of the privy-chamber; captain of the guards; one of the privy council, and high chancellor of England, and of the university of Oxford: who, to the great grief of his sovereign, and of all good men, ended this life religiously, after having lived unmarried to the age of fifty one, at his house in Holborn, on the 20th of November, A. D. 1591.

William Hatton, knight, his nephew by his sister's side, and by adoption his son and heir, most sorrowfully raised this tomb, as a mark of his duty.

On the left hand is the marble monument of William Herbert, earl of Pembroke, and his lady: and near it, that of John, duke of Lancaster, with this inscription:

Here sleeps in the Lord, John of Gant, so called from the city of the same name in Flanders, where he was born, fourth son of Edward the Third, king of England, and created by his father earl of Richmond. He was thrice married; first to Blanch, daughter and heiress of Henry duke of Lancaster, by her he received an immense inheritance, and became not only duke of Lancaster, but earl of Leicester, Lincoln, and Derby, of whose race are descended many emperors, kings, princes, and nobles. His second wife was Constance, who is here buried, daughter and heiress of Peter, king of Castile and Leon, in whose right he most * justly took the stile of king of Castile and Leon. She brought him one only daughter, Catherine, of whom, by Henry, are descended the kings of Spain. His third wife was Catherine, of a knight's family, a woman of great beauty, by whom he had a numerous progeny; from which is descended, by the mother's side, Henry the Seventh, the most prudent king of England, by whose most happy marriage with Elizabeth, daughter of Edward the Fourth, of the line of York, the two royal lines of Lancas-

* This is not true, for her legitimacy was with good reason contested.

ter and York are united, to the moſt deſired tranquillity of England.

The moſt illuſtrious prince, John, ſurnamed Plantagenet, king of Caſtile and Leon, duke of Lancaſter, earl of Richmond, Leiceſter, and Derby, lieutenant of Aquitain, high-ſteward of England, died in the twenty-firſt year of Richard II. A. D. 1398.

A little father, almoſt at the entrance of the choir, in a certain receſs, are two ſmall ſtone cheſts, one of which is thus inſcribed:

Here lies Seba, king of the Eaſt Saxons, who was converted to the faith by St. Erkenwald, biſhop of London, A. D. 677.

On the other:

Here lies Ethelred, king of the Angles, ſon of king Edgar.

On whom St. Duſtan is ſaid to have denounced vengeance, on his coronation-day, in the following words:

" In as much as thou haſt aſpired to the throne by
" the death of thy brother, againſt whoſe blood the
" Engliſh, along with thy infamous mother, con-
" ſpired, the ſword ſhall not paſs from thy houſe!
" but rage all the days of thy life, afflicting all thy
" generation, till thy kingdom ſhall be tranſlated to
" another, whoſe manner and language the people
" under thee knoweth not. Nor ſhall thy ſin be

" done away till after long chaftifement, nor the fin
" of thy mother, nor the fin of thofe men who af-
" fifted in thy wicked council."

All which came to pafs, as predicted by the faint; for, after being worfted and put to flight by Sueno king of the Danes, and his fon Canute; and at laft clofely befieged in London, he died miferably A. D. 1017, after he had reigned thirty-fix years in great difficulties.

There is befides in the middle of the church a tomb made of brafs, of fome bifhop of London, named William, who was in favour with Edward king of England, and afterwards made counfellor to king William. He was bifhop fixteen years, and died A. D. 1077. Near this, is the following infcription:

Virtue furvives the funeral.

To the memory of

Thomas Linacre, an eminent phyfician, John Caius placed this monument.

On the lower part of it is this infcription in gold letters:

Thomas Linacre, phyfician to king Henry VIII. a man learned in the Greek and Latin languages, and particularly fkilful in phyfick, by which he reftored many from a ftate of languifhment and defpair to life. He tranflated with extraordinary eloquence many of Galen's works into Latin; and publifhed, a little before his death, at the requeft of his friends, a very valuable book on the correct ftructure of the Latin tongue. He founded in perpetuity, in favour of ftudents in phyfick, two public lectures at Oxford, and one at Cambridge. In this city he brought about, by his own induftry, the eftablifhing of a college of phyficians, of which he was elected the firft prefident. He was a detefter of all fraud and deceit, and faithful in his friendfhips; equally dear to men of all ranks: he went into orders a few years before his death, and quitted this life full of years, and much lamented, A. D. 1524, on the twentieth of October.

There are many tombs in this church, but without any infcriptions. It has a very fine organ, which, at evening prayer, accompanied with other inftruments, is delightful.

In the fuburb to the weft, joined to the city by a continual row of palaces belonging to the chief nobility, of a mile in length, and laying on the fide next the Thames, is the fmall town of Weftminfter; originally called Thornep, from its thorn bufhes, but now Weftminfter, from its afpect and its monaftery. The church is remarkable for the coronation and burial of the kings of England. Upon this fpot is faid formerly to have ftood a temple of Apollo, which was thrown down by an earthquake in the time of Antoninus Pius; from the ruins of which Sebert king of the East-Saxons erected another to St. Peter: this was subverted by the Danes, and again renewed by bishop Dunstan, who gave it to a few monks. Afterwards, king Edward the Confessor built it entirely new, with the tenth of his whole revenue, to be the place of his own burial, and a convent of Benedictine monks; and enriched it with estates dispersed all over England.

In this church the following things are worthy of notice:

In the first choir, the tomb of Anne of Cleves, wife of Henry VIII. without any inscription.

On the opposite side are two stone sepulchres:

1. Edward, earl of Lancaster, brother of Edward I.
2. Ademar of Valence, earl of Pembroke, son of Ademar of Valence. Joining to these is, 3. that of Aveline, countess of Lancaster.

In the second choir is the chair on which the kings are seated, when they are crowned; in it is enclosed a stone, said to be that on which the patriarch Jacob slept, when he dreamed he saw a ladder reaching quite up into Heaven. Some Latin verses are written upon a tablet hanging near it; the sense of which is:

That if any faith is to be given to ancient chronicles

a stone of great note is inclosed in this chair, being the same on which the patriarch Jocob repofed, when he beheld the miraculous defcent of angels. Edward I. the Mars and Hector of England, having conquered Scotland, brought it from thence.

The tomb of Richard II. and his wife, of brafs, gilt, and thefe verfes written round it:

Perfect and prudent, Richard, by right the fecond,
   Vanquifh'd by fortune, lies here now graven in
      ftone,
True of his word, and thereto well refound:
   Seemly in perfon, and like to Homer, as one
In worldly prudence, and ever the church in one
Upheld and favour'd, cafting the proud to ground,
And all that would his royal ftate confound.

Without the tomb is this infcription:

Here lies king Richard, who perifhed by a cruel
      death, in the year 1369.
  To have been happy is additional mifery.

Near him is the monument of his queen, daughter of the emperor Wenceflaus.

On the left hand is the tomb of Edward I. with this infcription:

Here lies Edward I. who humbled the Scots. A. D. 1308. Be true to your engagements.

      He reigned forty-fix years.

The tomb of Edward III. of copper, guilt, with this epitaph:

Of English kings here lieth the beauteous flower,
Of all before past, and myrror to them shall sue:
A merciful king, of peace confervator,
The third Edward, &c.

Vid. DART. ii. 44.

Besides the tomb are these words:

Edward III. whose fame has reached to heaven. A. D. 1377. Fight for your country.

Here is shown his sword, eight feet in length, which they say he used in the conquest of France.

His queen's epitaph:

Here lies queen Phillippa, wife of Edward III. Learn to live. A. D. 1369.

At a little distance, the tomb of Henry V. with this legend:

Henry, the scourge of France, lies in this tomb. Virtue subdues all things. A. D. 1422.

Near this lies the coffin of Catherine, unburied, and to be opened by any one that pleases. On the outside is this inscription:

Fair Catherine is at length united to her lord. A. D. 1437. Shun idleness.

The tomb of Henry III. of brafs, gilt, with this epitaph:

Henry III. the founder of this cathedral. A.D. 1273.
War is delightful to the unexperienced.

It was this Henry, who, one hundred and fixty years after Edward the Confeffor had built this church, took it down, and raifed an entire new one of beautiful architecture, fupported by rows of marble columns, and its roof covered with fheets of lead, a work of fifty years before its completion. It has been much enlarged at the weft end by the abbots. After the expulfion of the monks, it experienced many changes; firft it had a dean and prebendaries; then a bifhop, who, having fquandred the revenues, refigned it again to a dean. In a little time, the monks with their abbot were re-inftated by queen Mary; but, they being foon ejected again by authority of parliament, it was converted into a cathedral church; nay into a feminary for the church, by queen Elizabeth, who inftituted there twelve prebendaries, an equal number of invalid foldiers, and forty fcholars; who at a proper time are elected into the univerfities, and are thence tranfplanted into the church and ftate.

Next to be feen is the tomb of Eleanor, daughter of Alphonfo king of Spain, and wife of Edward I. with this infcription:

This Eleanor was confort of Edward I.
A. D. 1298. Learn to die.

The tomb of Elizabeth, daughter of Henry VII.

In the middle of this chapel is the shrine of St. Edward, the last king of the Saxons. It is composed of marble in mosaic: round it runs this inscription in letters of gold:

> The venerable king, St. Edward the Confessor,
> A heroe adorned with every virtue.
> He died on the fifth of January, 1065,
> And mounted into Heaven.
> Lift up your hearts.

The third choir, of surprising splendor and elegance, was added to the east end by Henry VII. for a burying place for himself and his posterity. Here is to be seen his magnificent tomb, wrought of brass and marble, with this epitaph:

Here lies Henry VII. of that name, formerly king of England, son of Edmund earl of Richmond, who, ascending the throne on the twenty-second day of August, was crowned on the thirtieth of October following at Westminster, in the year of our Lord 1485. He died on the twenty-first of April, in the fifty third year of his age, after a reign of twenty two years, and eight months, wanting a day.

This monument is enclosed with rails of brass, with a long epitaph in Latin verse.

Under the same tomb lies buried Edward VI. king of England, son of Henry VIII. by Jane Seymour. He succeeded to his father when he was but nine years old, and died A. D. 1553, on the sixth of July, in the sixteenth year of his age, and of his reign the seventh, not without suspicion of poison.

Mary was proclaimed queen by the people, on the nineteenth of July, and died in November, 1558, and is buried in some corner of the same choir, without any inscription.

Queen Elizabeth.

Here lies queen Elizabeth, daughter of Edward IV. sister of king Edward V. wife of Henry VII. and the glorious mother of Henry VIII. she died in the Tower of London, on the eleventh of February, A. D. 1502, in the thirty-seventh year of her age.

Between the second and third choirs, in the sidechapels, are the tombs of Sebert king of the East-Saxons, who built this church with stone: and

Of Margaret of Richmond, mother of Henry VII. grandmother of Henry VIII. she gave this monastery to the monks of Winbourne *, who prea-

---

* This is a mistake; her epitaph says, *stipendia constituit tribus hoc cœnobio monachis & doctori grammatices apud* Wynbourne.

ched and taught grammar all England over, and appointed falaries to two profeffors of divinity, one at Oxford, another at Cambridge, where fhe founded two colleges, to Chrift, and to John his difciple. She died A. D. 1463, on the third of the calends of July.

And of Margaret countefs of Lenox, grandmother of James VI. king of Scotland.

William of Valance, half brother of Henry III.

The earl of Cornwall, brother of Edward III.

Upon another tomb is an honorary infcription for Frances, dutchefs of Suffolk: The fenfe of it is,

That titles, royal birth, riches, or a large family,
 are of no avail:
That all are tranfitory; virtue alone refifting the
 funeral pile.
That this lady was firft married to a duke, then to
 Stoke, a gentleman;
And laftly, by the grave efpoufed to CHRIST.

The next is the tomb of lord Ruffel, fon of the earl of Bedford, whofe lady compofed the following Greek and Latin verfes, and had them engraved on the marble:

How was I ftartled at the cruel feaft,
By death's rude hands in horrid manner dreft;
Such grief as fure no haplefs woman knew,
When thy pale image lay before my view.

Thy father's heir in beauteous form array'd
Like flowers in spring, and fair, like them to fade;
Leaving behind unhappy wretched me,
And all thy little orphan-progeny:
Alike the beauteous face, the comly air,
The tongue persuasive, and the actions fair,
Decay: so learning too in time shall waste:
But faith, chaste lovely faith, shall ever last.
The once bright glory of his house, the pride
Of all his country, dusty ruins hide:
Mourn, hapless orphans; mourn, once happy wife;
For when he dy'd, dy'd all the joys of life.
Pious and just, amidst a large estate,
He got at once the name of good and great.
He made no flatt'ring parasite his guest,
But ask'd the good companions to the feast.

Anne countess of Oxford, daughter of William Cecil, baron Burleigh, and lord treasurer.

Philippa, daughter and coheiress of John lord Mohun of Dunster, wife of Edward duke of York.

Frances countess of Sussex, of the antient family of Sidney.

Thomas Bromley, chancellor to queen Elizabeth.

The earl of Bridgewater *, lord Dawbney, lord chamberlain to Henry VII. and his lady.

And thus much for WESTMINSTER.

* Sir Giles Dawbney; he was not earl of Bridgewater, nor a lord.

There are many other churches in this city, but none so remarkable for the tombs of persons of distinction.

Near to this church is Westminster-hall, where, besides the sessions of parliament, which are often held there, are the courts of justice; and at stated times are heard their trials in law, or concerning the king's patrimony; or in chancery, which moderates the severity of the common law by equity. Till the time of Henry I. the prime court of justice was moveable, and followed the King's court, but he enacted, by the Magna Charta, that the Common Pleas should no longer attend his court, but be held at some determined place. The present hall was built by king Richard II. in the place of an ancient one which he caused to be taken down. He made it part of his habitation (for at that time the kings of England determined causes in their own proper person, and from the days of Edward the Confessor, had their palace adjoining); till, above sixty years since, upon its being burnt, Henry VIII. removed the royal residence to White-hall, situated in the neighbourhood, which a little before was the house of Cardinal Wolsey: this palace is truly royal; enclosed on one side by the Thames, on the other by a park, which connects it with St. James's, another royal palace.

In the chamber where the parliament is usually held, the seats and wainscot are made of wood, the growth of Ireland; said to have that occult quality, that all poisonous animals are driven away by it: and it is affirmed for certain, that in Ireland there are neither serpents, toads, nor any other venomous creature to be found.

Near this palace are seen an immense number of swans, who wander up and down the river for some miles, in great security; no body daring to molest, much less kill any of them, under penalty of a considerable fine.

In Whitehall are the following things worthy of observation:

I. The royal library, well stored with Greek, Latin, Italian and French books: amongst the rest, a little one in French, upon parchment, in the hand writing of the present reigning queen Elizabeth, thus inscribed:

To the most high, puissant, and redoubted prince, Henry VIII. of the name, king of England, France and Ireland, Defender of the faith:
Elizabeth, his most humble daughter,
Health and obedience.

All these books are bound in velvet of different colours, though chiefly red, with clasps of gold and silver; some have pearls, and precious stones, set in their bindings.

II. Two little silver cabinets of exquisite work, in which the queen keeps her paper, and which she uses for writing boxes.

III. The queen's bed, ingeniously composed of woods of different colours, with quilts of silk, velvet, gold, silver, and embroidery.

IV. A little chest ornamented all over with pearls, in which the queen keeps her bracelets, ear-rings, and other things of extraordinary value.

V. Christ's passion, in painted glass.

VI. Portraits: among which are, queen Elizabeth; at sixteen years old; Henry, Richard, Edward, kings of England; Rosamond; Lucrece, a Grecian bride, in her nuptial habit; the genealogy of the kings of England; a picture of king Edward VI. representing at first sight something quite deformed, till by looking through a small hole in the cover, which is put over it, you see it in its true proportions; Charles V. emperor; Charles Emanuel duke of Sovoy, and Catherine of Spain, his wife; Ferdinand duke of Florence, with his daughters; one of Philip king of Spain, when he came into England and married Mary; Henry VII. Henry VIII. and his mother: besides many more of illustrious men and women; and a picture of the siege of Malta.

VII. A small hermitage, half hid in a rock, finely carved in wood.

VIII. Variety of emblems, on paper, cut in the shape of shields, with mottoes, used by the nobility at tilts and tournaments, hung up here for a memorial.

IX. Different inftruments of mufic, upon one of which two perfons may perform at the fame time.

X. A piece of clock work, an Ethiop riding upon a Rhinoceros, with four attendants, who all make their obeifance, when it ftrikes the hour; thefe are all put into motion by winding up the machine.

At the entrance into the park from Whitehall is this infcription:

* The fifherman who has been wounded, learns,
though late, to beware;
But the unfortunate Actæon always preffes on.
The chafte virgin naturally pitied:
But the powerful goddefs revenged the wrong.
Let Actæon fall a prey to his dogs,
An example to youth,
A difgrace to thofe that belong to him!
May Diana live the care of heaven;
The delight of mortals;
The fecurity of thofe that belong to her!

* This romantic infcription probably alluded to Philip II. who woed the queen after her fifter's death; and to the deftruction of his armada.

In this park is great plenty of deer.

In a garden joining to this palace, there is a jet d'eau, with a fun dial, which while ſtrangers are looking at, a quantity of water, forced by a wheel, which the gardener turns at a diſtance, through a number of little pipes, plentifully ſprinkles thoſe that are ſtanding round.

Guild-hall, a fine ſtructure, built by Thomas Knowles: here are to be ſeen the ſtatues of two giants, ſaid to have aſſiſted the Engliſh when the Romans made war upon them; Corinius of Britain, and Gogmagog of Albion. Beneath upon a table the titles of Charles V. emperor, are written in letters of gold.

The government of London is this: the city is divided into twenty-five regions, or wards; the council is compoſed of twenty four aldermen, one of which preſides over every ward. And whereas of old, the chief magiſtrate was a portreve, i. e. governor of the city: Richard I. appointed two bailiffs; inſtead of which king John gave a power by grant, of chuſing annually a mayor, from any of the twelve principal companies, and to name two ſheriffs, one of which to be called the king's, the other, the city's. It is ſcarce credible how this city increaſed, both in public and private buildings, upon eſtabliſhing this form of government. Vide Cambden's Britan. Middleſex.

It is worthy of obfervation, that every year upon St. Bartholomew's day, when the fair is held, it is ufual for the mayor, attended by the twelve principal aldermen, to walk in a neighbouring field, dreffed in his fcarlet gown, and about his neck a golden chain, to which is hung a golden fleece *, and befides, that particular ornament †, which diftinguifhes the moft noble order of the garter. During the year of his magiftracy, he is obliged to live fo magnificently, that foreigner or native, without any expence, is free, if he can find a chair empty, to dine at his table, where there is always the greateft plenty. When the mayor goes out of the precincts of the city, a fcepter, a fword, and a cap, are borne before him, and he is followed by the principal aldermen in fcarlet gowns, with gold chains ; himfelf and they on horfeback : upon their arrival at a place appointed for that purpofe, where a tent is pitched, the mob begin to wreftle before them, two at a time ; the conquerors receive rewards from the magiftrates. After this is over, a parcel of live rabits are turned loofe among the crowd, which are purfued by a number of boys, who endeavour to catch them, with all the noife they can make. While we were at this fhow, one of our

* This probably alluded to the woollen manufacture; Stow mentions his riding through the Cloth Fair, on the Eve of St. Bartholomew, p. 651.

† The collar of SS.

company, Tobias Salander, doctor of physic, had his pocket picked of his purse, with nine crowns du soleil, which without doubt was so cleverly taken from him, by an Englishman, who always kept very close to him, that the doctor did not in the least perceive it.

The Castle, or Tower of London, called Bringwin, and Tourgwin, in Welsh, from its whiteness, is encompassed by a very deep and broad ditch, as well as a double wall very high. In the middle of the whole is that very antient and very strong tower, enclosed with four others, which, in the opinion of some, was built by Julius Cæsar. Upon entering the tower, we were obliged to quit our swords at the gate, and deliver them to the guard. When we were introduced, we were shewn above a hundred pieces of arras belonging to the crown, made of gold, silver, and silk; several saddles covered with velvet of different colours; an immense quantity of bed-furniture, such as canopies, and the like, some of them most richly ornamented with pearl; some royal dresses, so extremely magnificent, as to raise any one's admiration at the sums they must have cost. We were next led into the armoury, in which are these particularities: spears, out of which you may shoot; shields, that will give fire four times; a great many rich halberds, commonly called partuisans, with which the guard defend the royal person in battle; some lances, covered with red and green velvet, and the body-armour of

Henry VIII.; many, and very beautiful arms, as well for men, as for horses in horse-fights; the lance of Charles Brandon duke of Suffolk, three spans thick; two pieces of cannon, the one fires three, the other seven balls at a time; two others made of wood, which the English had at the siege of Boulogne, in France. And by this stratagem, without which they could not have succeeded, they struck a terror into the inhabitants, as at the appearance of artillery, and the town was surrendered upon articles; nineteen cannon, of a thicker make than ordinary, and in a room apart; thirty-six of a smaller; other cannon for chain-shot; and balls proper to bring down masts of ships. Cross-bows, bows and arrows, of which to this day the English make great use in their exercises: but who can relate all that is to be seen here? Eight or nine men, employed by the year, are scarce sufficient to keep all the arms bright.

The mint for coining money is in the tower.

N. B. It is to be noted, that when any of the nobility are sent hither, on the charge of high crimes, punishable with death, such as treason, &c. they seldom or never recover their liberty. Here was beheaded Anna Bolen, wife of king Henry VIII. and lies buried in the chapel, but without any inscription: and queen Elizabeth was kept prisoner here by her sister queen Mary, at whose death she was enlarged, and by right called to the throne.

On coming out of the tower, we were led to a small houſe cloſe by, where are kept variety of creatures, viz. three lioneſſes, one lion of great ſize, called Edward VI. from his having been born in that reign ; a tyger ; a lynx ; a wolf exceſſively old ; this is a very ſcarce animal in England, ſo that their ſheep and cattle ſtray about in great numbers, free from any danger, though without any body to keep them ; there is beſides, a porcupine, and an eagle. All theſe creatures are kept in a remote place, fitted up for the purpoſe with wooden lattices at the queen's expence.

Near to this tower, is a large open ſpace : on the higheſt part of it is erected a wooden ſcaffold, for the execution of noble criminals ; upon which they ſay, three princes of England, the laſt of their families, have been beheaded for high treaſon ; on the bank of the Thames cloſe by, are a great many cannon, ſuch chiefly as are uſed at ſea.

The next thing worthy of note, is the Royal Exchange, ſo named by queen Elizabeth, built by Sir Thomas Greſham, citizen, for public ornament, and the convenience of merchants. It has a great effect, whether you conſider the ſtatelineſs of the building, the aſſemblage of different nations, or the quantities of merchandiſe. I ſhall ſay nothing of the hall belonging to the Hans ſociety ; or of the conveyance of water to all parts of the town by ſubterraneous pipes, nor the beautiful conduits and cifterns for the reception of it; nor of the rifing of water out of the Thames by a wheel, invented a few years fince by a German.

Bridewell, at prefent the houfe of correction: it was built in fix weeks for the reception of the emperor Charles V.

A Hall, built by a cobler, and beftowed on the city, where are expofed to fale three times in a week, corn, wool, cloth, fruits, and the like.

Without the city are fome Theatres, where Englifh actors reprefent almoft every day tragedies and comedies to very numerous audiences; thefe are concluded with excellent mufic, variety of dances, and the exceffive applaufe of thofe that are prefent.

Not far from one of thefe theatres, which are all built of wood, lies the royal barge, clofe to the river; it has two fplendid cabins, beautifully ornamented with glafs windows, painting and gilding; it is kept upon dry ground, and fheltered from the weather.

There is ftill another place, built in the form of a theatre, which ferves for the baiting of bulls and bears; they are faftened behind, and then worried by great Englifh bull-dogs, but not without great rifque to the dogs, from the horns of the one, and the teeth of the other; and it fometimes happens they are killed upon the spot; fresh ones are immediately supplied in the places of those that are wounded, or tired. To this entertainment, there often follows that of whipping a blinded bear, which is performed by five or six men, standing circularly with whips, which they exercise upon him without any mercy, as he cannot escape from them because of his chain; he defends himself with all his force and skill, throwing down all who come within his reach, and are not active enough to get out of it, and tearing the whips out of their hands, and breaking them. At these spectacles, and every where else, the English are constantly smoaking tobacco; and in this manner; they have pipes on purpose made of clay, into the farther end of which they put the herb, so dry that it may be rubbed into powder, and putting fire to it, they draw the smoak into their mouths, which they puff out again, through their nostrils, like funnels, along with it plenty of phlegm and defluxion from the head. In these theatres, fruits, such as apples, pears and nuts, according to the season, are carried about to be sold, as well as ale and wine.

There are fifteen colleges, within and without the city, nobly built, with beautiful gardens adjoining. Of these the three principal are:

I. The Temple, inhabited formerly by the Knights Templars: it seems to have taken its name from the old temple, or church, which has a round tower added to it, under which lie buried thofe kings of Denmark, that reigned in England.

II. Gray's Inn. And,

III. Lincoln's Inn.

In thefe colleges numbers of the young nobility, gentry, and others, are educated, and chiefly in the ftudy of phyfic, for very few apply themfelves to that of the law: they are allowed a very good table, and filver cups to drink out of. Once a perfon of diftinction, who could not help being furprifed at the great number of cups, faid, "He
" fhould have thought it more fuitable to the life of
" ftudents, if they had ufed rather glafs, or ear-
" then-ware, than filver." The college anfwered,
" They were ready to make him a prefent of all
" their plate, provided he would undertake to fupply
" them with all the glafs, and earthen-ware, they
" fhould have a demand for; fince it was very
" likely he would find the expence, from conftant
" breaking, exceed the value of the filver."

The ftreets in this city are very handfome and clean; but that which is named from the goldfmiths who inhabit it, furpaffes all the reft: there is in it a gilt tower, with a fountain that plays. Near it, on the farther fide, is a handfome houfe, built by a goldfmith, and prefented by him to the city. There are befides to be feen in this ftreet, as in all others where there are goldsmiths' shops, all sorts of gold and silver vessels exposed to sale; as well as ancient and modern medals, in such quantities as must surprize a man the first time he sees and considers them.

Fitz-Stevens, a writer of English history, reckoned in his time in London, one hundred and twenty-seven parish churches, and thirteen belonging to convents: he mentions besides, that upon a review there of men able to bear arms, the people brought into the field under their colours, forty thousand foot, and twenty thousand horse. Vide Cambden's Britan. Middlesex.

The best oysters are sold here in great quantities.

Every body knows that English cloth is much approved of, for the goodness of the materials, and imported into all the kingdoms and provinces of Europe.

We were shewn, at the house of Leonard Smith, a taylor, a most perfect looking-glass, ornamented with gold, pearl, silver, and velvet, so richly as to be estimated at five hundred ecus du soleil. We saw at the same place the hippocamp and eagle stone, both very curious and rare.

And thus much of LONDON.

Upon taking the air down the river, the firſt thing that ſtruck us, was the ſhip of that noble pirate, ſir Francis Drake, in which he is ſaid to have ſurrounded this globe of earth. On the left hand lies Ratcliffe, a conſiderable ſuburb: on the oppoſite ſhore is fixed a long pole with rams-horns upon it, the intention of which was vulgarly ſaid to be, a reflection upon wilful and contented cuckolds.

We arrived next at the royal palace of Greenwich, reported to have been originally built by Humphrey duke of Glouceſter, and to have received very magnificent additions from Henry VII. It was here Elizabeth, the preſent queen, was born, and here ſhe generally reſides; particularly in ſummer, for the delightfulneſs of its ſituation. We were admitted by an order Mr. Rogers had procured from the lord chamberlain, into the preſence-chamber, hung with rich tapeſtry, and the floor after the Engliſh faſhion, ſtrewed with * hay, through which the queen commonly paſſes in her way to chapel: at the door ſtood a gentleman dreſſed in velvet, with a gold chain, whoſe office was to introduce to the queen any perſon of diſtinction, that came to wait on her: it was Sunday, when there is uſually the greateſt attendance of nobility. In the ſame hall were the archbiſhop of Canterbury, the biſhop of London, a great number of counſellors of ſtate, of-

---

* He probably means ruſhes.

ficers of the crown, and gentlemen, who waited the queen's coming out; which she did from her own apartment, when it was time to go to prayers, attended in the following manner:

First went gentlemen, barons, earls, knights of the garter, all richly dressed and bareheaded; next came the chancellor, bearing the seals in a red-silk purse, between two; one of which carried the royal scepter, the other the sword of state, in a red scabbard, studded with golden fleurs de lis, the point upwards: next came the queen, in the sixty-fifth year of her age, as we were told, very majestic; her face oblong, fair, but wrinkled; her eyes small, yet black and pleasant; her nose a little hooked; her lips narrow, and her teeth black; (a defect the English seem subject to, from their too great use of sugar) she had in her ears two pearls, with very rich drops; she wore false hair, and that red; upon her head she had a small crown, reported to be made of some of the gold of the celebrated Lunebourg table *: her bosom was uncovered, as all the English ladies have it, till they marry; and she had on a necklace of exceeding fine jewels; her hands were small, her fingers long, and her stature neither tall nor low; her air was stately, her manner of speaking mild and obliging. That day she was dressed in white silk, bordered with pearls of the size of beans, and over it a mantle of

---

* At this distance of time, it is difficult to say what this was.

black silk, shot with silver threads; her train was very long, the end of it borne by a marchioness; instead of a chain, she had an oblong collar of gold and jewels. As she went along in all this state and magnificence, she spoke very graciously, first to one, then to another, whether foreign ministers, or those who attended for different reasons, in English, French, and Italian; for, besides being well skilled in Greek, Latin, and the languages I have mentioned, she is mistress of Spanish, Scotch and Dutch: whoever speaks to her, it is kneeling; now and then she raises some with her hand. While we were there, W. Slawata, a Bohemian baron, had letters to present to her; and she, after pulling off her glove, gave him her right hand to kiss, sparkling with rings and jewels, a mark of particular favour: whereever she turned her face, as she was going along, every body fell down on * their knees. The ladies of the court followed next to her, very handsome and well shaped, and for the most part dressed in white; she was guarded on each side by the gentlemen pensioners, fifty in number, with gilt battleaxes. In the antichapel next the hall where we were, petitions were presented to her, and she re-

* Her father had been treated with the same deference. It is mentioned by Fox in his acts and monuments, that when the lord chancellor went to apprehend queen Catherine Parr, he spoke to the king on his knees.

King James I. suffered his courtiers to omit it.

BACON's Papers, Vol. II. p. 516.

ceived them moſt gracicuſly, which occaſioned the acclamation of, LONG LIVE QUEEN ELIZABETH! ſhe anſwered it with, I THANK YOU MY GOOD PEOPLE. In the chapel was excellent muſic; as ſoon as it, and the ſervice was over, which ſcarce exceeded half an hour, the queen returned in the ſame ſtate and order, and prepared to go to dinner. But while ſhe was ſtill at prayers, we ſaw her table ſet out with the following ſolemnity:

A gentleman entered the room bearing a rod, and along with him another who had a table-cloth, which, after they had both kneeled three times with the utmoſt veneration, he ſpread upon the table, and after kneeling again, they both retired. Then came two others, one with the rod again, the other with a ſalt-ſeller, a plate and bread; when they had kneeled, as the others had done, and placed what was brought upon the table, they too retired with the ſame ceremonies performed by the firſt. At laſt came an unmarried lady (we were told ſhe was a counteſs) and along with her a married one, bearing a taſting-knife; the former was dreſſed in white ſilk, who, when ſhe had proſtrated herſelf three times in the moſt graceful manner, approached the table, and rubbed the plates with bread and ſalt, with as much awe, as if the queen had been preſent: when they had waited there a little while, the yeomen of the guards entered, bareheaded, clothed in ſcarlet, with a golden roſe upon their backs, bringing in at each turn a courſe of twenty-four dishes, served in plate, most of it gilt; these dishes were received by a gentleman in the same order they were brought, and placed upon the table, while the lady-taster gave to each of the guard a mouthful to eat, of the particular dish he had brought for fear of any poison. During the time that this guard, which consists of the tallest and stoutest men that can be found in all England, being carefully selected for this service, were bringing dinner, twelve trumpets and two kettle-drums made the hall ring for half an hour together. At the end of all this ceremonial a number of unmarried ladies appeared, who, with particular solemnity, lifted the meat off the table, and conveyed it into the queen's inner and more private chamber, where, after she had chosen for herself, the rest goes to the ladies of the court.

The queen dines and sups alone with very few attendants; and it is very seldom that any body, foreigner or native, is admitted at that time, and then only at the intercession of somebody in power.

Near this palace is the queen's park, stocked with deer: such parks are common throughout England, belonging to those that are distinguished either for their rank or riches. In the middle of this is an old square tower, called **Mirefleur**, supposed to be that mentioned in the romance of Amadis de Gaul; and joining to it a plain, where knights and other gentlemen ufe to meet, at fet times and holidays, to exercife on horfeback.

We left London in a coach, in order to fee the remarkable places in its neighbourhood.

The firft was Theobalds, belonging to lord Burleigh the treafurer: in the gallery was painted the genealogy of the kings of England; from this place one goes into the garden, encompaffed with a ditch full of water, large enough for one to have the pleafure of going in a boat, and rowing between the fhrubs; here are great variety of trees and plants; labyrinths made with a great deal of labour; a jet d'eau, with its bafon of white marble; and columns and pyramids of wood and other materials up and down the garden. After feeing thefe, we were led by the gardener into the fummer-houfe, in the lower part of which, built femicircularly, are the twelve Roman emperors in white marble, and a table of touchftone; the upper part of it is fet round with cifterns of lead, into which the water is conveyed through pipes, fo that fifh may be kept in them, and in fummer time they are very convenient for bathing; in another room for entertainment very near this, and joined to it by a little bridge, was an oval table of red marble. We were not admitted to fee the apartments of this palace, there being nobody to fhew it, as the family was in town attending the funeral of their lord *.

* Lord treafurer Burleigh died Auguft 4, 1598

Hodfdon, a village.

Ware, a market town.

Puckeridge, a village; this was the firſt place where we obſerved that the beds at inns were made by the waiters.

Camboritum, Cantabrigium, and Cantabrigia, now called Cambridge, a celebrated town, ſo named from the river Cam, which after waſhing the weſtern ſide, playing through iſlands, turns to the eaſt, and divides the town into two parts, which are joined by a bridge; whence its modern name: formerly it had the Saxon one of Grantbridge. Beyond this bridge is an antient and large caſtle, ſaid to be built by the Danes: on this ſide, where far the greater part of the town ſtands, all is ſplendid; the ſtreets fine, the churches numerous, and thoſe ſeats of the Muſes, the colleges, moſt beautiful; in theſe a great number of learned men are ſupported, and the ſtudies of all polite ſciences and languages flouriſh.

I think proper to mention ſome few things about the foundation of this Univerſity, and its colleges. Cantaber, a Spaniard, is thought to have firſt inſtituted this academy, 375 years before Chriſt; and Sebert king of the Eaſt-Angles, to have reſtored it, A. D. 630. It was afterwards ſubverted in the confuſion under the Danes, and lay long neglected;

till upon the Norman conqueſt every thing began to brighten up again: from that time, inns and halls for the convenient lodging of ſtudents began to be built, but without any revenues annexed to them.

The firſt college, called Peter-Houſe, was built and endowed by Hugh Balſam, biſhop of Ely, A. D. 1280; and in imitation of him, Richard Badew, with the aſſiſtance of Elizabeth Burk, counteſs of Clare and Ulſter, founded Clare Hall, in 1326; Mary de St. Paul counteſs of Pembroke, Pembroke Hall, in 1343; the Monks of Corpus Chriſti, the college of the ſame name, though it has beſides that of Bennet; John Craudene, Trinity Hall, 1354; Edmond Gonville in 1348, and John Caius, a phyſician in our times, Gonville and Caius college; king Henry VI. King's College, in 1441; adding to it a chapel, that may juſtly claim a place among the moſt beautiful buildings in the world; on its right ſide is a fine library, where we ſaw the Book of Pſalms in manuſcript upon parchment, four ſpans in length, and three broad, taken from the Spaniards at the ſiege of Cadiz, and thence brought into England with other rich ſpoils. Margaret of Anjou, his wife, founded Queen's College, 1448, at the ſame time that John Alcock, biſhop of Ely, built Jeſus College; Robert Woodlarke, Catherine Hall; Margaret of Richmond, mother of king Henry VII. Chriſt's and St. John's Colleges, about 1506; Thomas Audley, chancellor of England, Magdalen College, much increaſed ſince both in buildings and revenue by Chriftopher Wray, lord chief juftice; and the moft potent king Henry VIII. erected Trinity College for religion and polite letters; in its chapel is the tomb of Dr. Wintacre, with an infcription in gold letters upon marble; Emanuel College built in our own times by the moft honourable and prudent Sir Walter Mildmay, one of her majefty's privy council: and laftly, Sidney College, now firft building by the executors of the lady * Frances Sidney, countefs of Suffex.

We muft note here, that there is a certain fect in England, called Puritans: thefe, according to the doctrine of the church of Geneva, reject all ceremonies antiently held, and admit of neither organs nor tombs in their places of worfhip, and entirely abhor all difference in rank among churchmen, fuch as bifhops, deans, &c. they were firft named Puritans by the Jefuit Sandys. They do not live feparate, but mix with thofe of the church of England in the colleges.

Potton, a village.

Ampthill, a town; here we faw immenfe numbers of rabbits, which are reckoned as good as hares, and are very well tafted.

* She was the daughter, fifter and aunt, of thofe eminent knights, Sir William, Sir Henry, and Sir Philip Sidney.

We paſſed through the towns of Woburn, Leighton, Aileſbury, and Wheatley.

Oxonium, Oxford, the famed Athens of England; that glorious ſeminary of learning and wiſdom, whence religion, politeneſs, and letters, are abundantly diſperſed into all parts of the kingdom: the town is remarkably fine, whether you conſider the elegance of its private buildings, the magnificence of its public ones, or the beauty and wholeſomeneſs of its ſituation; which is on a plain, encompaſſed in ſuch a manner with hills ſhaded with wood, as to be ſheltered on the one hand from the ſickly ſouth, and on the other from the bluſtering weſt, but open to the eaſt that blows ſerene weather, and to the north the preventer of corruption; from which, in the opinion of ſome, it formerly obtained the appellation of Belloſitum. This town is watered by two rivers, the Cherwell, and the Iſis, vulgarly called the Ouſe; and though theſe ſtreams join in the ſame channel, yet the Iſis runs more entire, and with more rapidity towards the ſouth, retaining its name, till it meets the Thame, which it ſeems long to have ſought, at Wallingford; thence called by the compound name of Thames, it flows the prince of all Britiſh rivers; of whom we may juſtly ſay, as the antients did of the Euphrates, that it both ſows and waters England.

The colleges in this famous Univerſity are as follow:

In the reign of Henry III. Walter Merton, bishop of Rochester, removed the college he had founded in Surrey, 1274, to Oxford, enriched it, and named it Merton College; and soon after William archdeacon of Durham, restored with additions that building of Alfred's, now called University College; in the reign of Edward I. John Baliol, king of Scotland, or, as some will have it, his parents, founded Baliol College; in the reign of Edward II. Walter Stapleton, bishop of Exeter, founded Exeter College, and Hart Hall: and, in imitation of him, the king, King's College, commonly called Oriel; and St. Mary's Hall; next Philippa, wife of Edward III. built Queen's College; and Simon Islip archbishop of Canterbury, Canterbury College; William Wickham, bishop of Winchester, raised that magnificent structure, called New College; Magdalen College was built by William Wainflet, bishop of Winchester, a noble edifice, finely situated, and delightful for its walks: at the same time Humphrey duke of Gloucester, that great encourager of learning, built the divinity school very splendidly, and over it a library, to which he gave an hundred and twenty-nine very choice books, purchased at a great price from Italy, but the public has long since been robbed of the use of them by the avarice of particulars: Lincoln College; All-Souls College; St. Bernard's College; Brazen-Nose College, founded by William Smith, bishop of Lincoln, in the reign of Henry VII. its revenues were augmented by Alexander Nowel, dean of St. Paul's, London;

upon the gate of this college is fixed a nofe of brafs: Corpus Chrifti College built by Richard Fox bifhop of Winchefter: under his picture in the college chapel are lines importing that it is the exact reprefentation of his perfon and drefs.

Chrift's Church, the largeft and moft elegant of them all, was begun on the ground of St. Fridefwide's Monaftery, by Thomas Wolfey, cardinal of York; to which Henry VIII. joined Canterbury College, fettled great revenues upon it, and named it Chrift's Church: the fame great prince, out of his own treafury, to the dignity of the town, and ornament of the univerfity, made the one a bifhoprick, and inftituted profefforfhips in the other.

Jefus College, built by Hugh Price Doctor of Laws.

That fine edifice, the public fchools, was entirly raifed by queen Mary, and adorned with various infcriptions.

Thus far of the colleges and halls, which for the beauty of their buildings, their rich endowments, and copious libraries, excell all the academies in the chriftian world. We fhall add a little of the academies themfelves, and thofe that inhabit them.

Thefe ftudents lead a life almoft monaftic; for as the Monks had nothing in the world to do, but when they had said their prayers at stated hours, to employ themselves in instructive studies, no more have these. They are divided into three tables: the first is called the fellows table, to which are admitted earls, barons, gentlemen, doctors, and masters of arts, but very few of the latter; this is more plentifully and expensively served than the others: the second is for masters of arts, bachelors, some gentlemen, and eminent citizens: the third for people of low condition. While the rest are at dinner or supper in a great hall, where they are all assembled, one of the students reads aloud the bible, which is placed on a desk in the middle of the hall, and this office every one of them takes upon himself in his turn; as soon as grace is said after each meal, every one is a liberty, either to retire to his own chambers, or to walk in the college garden, there being none that has not a delightful one. Their habit is almost the same as that of the jesuits, their gowns reaching down to their ankles, sometimes lined with fur; they wear square caps; the doctors, masters of arts, and professors, have another kind of gown that distinguishes them: every student of any considerable standing has a key to the college library, for no college is without one.

In an out part of the town are the remains of a pretty large fortification, but quite in ruins. We were entertained at supper with an excellent concert, composed of variety of instruments.

The next day we went as far as the royal palace of Woodstock, where king Ethelred formerly held a parliament, and enacted certain laws. This palace abounding in magnificence was built by Henry I. to which he joined a very large park, enclosed with a wall, according to John Rosse the first park in England. In this very palace the present reigning queen Elizabeth, before she was confined to the tower, was kept prisoner by her sister Mary; while she was detained here in the utmost peril of her life, she wrote with a piece of charcoal the following verses, composed by herself, upon a window shutter:

O Fortune! how thy restless wavering state
   Hath fraught with cares my troubled wit!
Witness this present prison whither fate
   Hath born me, and the joys I quit.
Thou causedest the guilty to be loosed
From bands, wherewith are innocents enclosed;
   Causing the guiltless to be strait reserved,
And freeing those that death had well deserved:
But by her envy can be nothing wrought,
So God send to my foes all they have thought.
               ELIZABETH Prisoner.

A. D. M.D.LV.

Not far from this palace are to be seen near a spring of the brightest water the ruins of the habitation of Rosamond Clifford, whose exquisite beauty so entirely captivated the heart of King Henry II.

that he loft the thought of all other women; fhe is
faid to have been poifoned at laft by the queen. All
that remains of her tomb of ftone, the letters of
which are almoft worn out, is the following:

* * * * * * * * * * * * *Adorent,*
Utque tibi detur requies Rofamunda precamur.

The rhiming epitaph following, was probably
the performance of fome monk:

Hic jacet in tumbâ Rofamundi non Rofamunda,
Non redolet fed olet, quæ redolere folet.

Returning from hence to Oxford, after dinner
we proceeded on our journey, and paffed through
Ewhelme, a royal palace, in which fome alms-
people are fupported by an allowance from the
crown.

Nettlebed, a village.

We went through the little town of Henley;
from hence the Chiltern hills bear north in a continued ridge, and divide the counties of Oxford
and Buckingham.

We paffed Maidenhead.

Windfor, a royal caftle, fuppofed to have been
begun by king Arthur, its buildings much increafed

by Edward III. The situation is entirely worthy of being a royal residence, a more beautiful being scarce to be found: for, from the brow of a gentle rising, it enjoys the prospect of an even and green country; its front commands a valley extended every way, and chequered with arable lands and pasturage, clothed up and down with groves, and watered by that gentlest of rivers the Thames; behind rise several hills, but neither steep, nor very high, crowned with woods, and seeming designed by Nature herself for the purpose of hunting.

The kings of England, invited by the deliciousness of the place, very often retire hither; and here was born the conqueror of France, the glorious king Edward III., who built the Castle new from the ground, and thoroughly fortified it with trenches, and towers of square stone, and having soon after subdued in battle John king of France, and David king of Scotland, he detained them both prisoners here at the same time. This Castle, besides being the royal palace, and having some magnificent tombs of the kings of England, is famous for the ceremonies belonging to the Knights of the Garter: this Order was instituted by Edward III., the same who triumphed so illustriously over John king of France. The Knights of the Garter are strictly chosen for their military virtues, and antiquity of family: They are bound by solemn oath and vow to mutual and perpetual friendship among themselves, and to the not avoiding any danger whatever,

or even death itfelf, to fupport, by their joint endeavours, the honour of the Society: they are ftiled, Companions of the Garter, from their wearing below the left knee a purple garter, infcribed in letters of gold, with HONI SOIT QUI MAL Y PENSE, i. e. *Evil to him that evil thinks.* This they wear upon the left leg, in memory of one which happening to untie, was let fall by a great lady, paffionately beloved by Edward, while fhe was dancing, and was immediately fnatched up by the king; who, to do honour to the lady, not out of any trifling galantry, but with a moft ferious and honourable purpofe, dedicated it to the legs of the moft diftinguifhed nobility. The ceremonies of this Society are celebrated every year at Windfor on St. George's day, the tutelar Saint of the Order, the king prefiding; and the cuftom is, that the Knights Companions fhould hang up their helmet and fhield, with their arms blazoned on it, in fome confpicuous part of the church.

There are three principal and very large courts in Windfor Caftle, which give great pleafure to the beholders: the firft is enclofed with moft elegant buildings of white ftone, flat roofed, and covered with lead; here the Knights of the Garter are lodged; in the middle is a detached houfe, remarkable for its high tower, which the governor inhabits. In this is the public kitchen, well furnifhed with proper utenfils, befides a fpacious dining-room, where all the poor Knights eat at the fame table, for into this Society of the Garter, the king and fovereign elects, at his own choice, certain perfons, who muft be gentlemen of three defcents, and fuch as, for their age and the ftraitnefs of their fortunes, are fitter for faying their prayers than for the fervice of war; to each of them is affigned a penfion of eighteen pounds per annum and clothes: the chief inftitution of fo magnificent a foundation is, that they fhould fay their daily prayers to God for the king's fafety, and the happy adminiftration of the kingdom, to which purpofe they attend the fervice, meeting twice every day at chapel. The left fide of this court is ornamented by a moft magnificent chapel of one hundred and thirty-four paces in length, and fixteen in breadth; in this are eighteen feats fitted up in the time of Edward III. for an equal number of Knights: this venerable building is decorated with the noble monuments of Edward IV., Henry VI., and VIII., and of his wife queen Jane. It receives from royal liberality the annual income of two thoufand pounds, and that ftill much increafed by the munificence of Edward III. and Henry VII. The greateft princes in Chriftendom have taken it for the higheft honour to be admitted into the Order of the Garter; and fince its firft inftitution about twenty kings, befides thofe of England, who are the fovereigns of it, not to mention dukes and perfons of the greateft figure, have been of it. It confifts of twenty-fix Companions.

In the inward choir of the chapel are hung up

Thomas Wolsey.

Bp. of Lincoln 1513. Abp. of York 1514...
Cardinal 1515. Lord Chancellor 1516. Ob 1530...
at. 59...

fixteen coats of arms, fwords, and banners; among which are thofe of Charles V. and Rodolphus II., Emperors; of Philip of Spain; Henry III. of France; Frederic II. of Denmark, &c.; of Cafimir Count Palatine of the Rhine; and other Chriftian princes who have been chofen into this Order.

In the back choir, or additional chapel, are fhewn preparations made by Cardinal Wolfey, who was afterwards capitally punifhed*, for his own tomb; confifting of eight large brazen columns placed round it, and nearer the tomb four others in the fhape of candlefticks; the tomb itfelf is of white and black marble; all which are referved, according to report, for the funeral of queen Elizabeth; the expences already made for that purpofe are eftimated at upwards of 60,000l. In the fame chapel is the furcoat † of Edward III., and the tomb of Edward Fines Earl of Lincoln, Baron Clinton and Say, Knight of the moft noble Order of the Garter, and formerly Lord High Admiral of England.

The fecond Court of Windfor Caftle ftands upon higher ground, and is enclofed with walls of great

* This was a ftrange blunder to be made fo near the time, about fo remarkable a perfon, unlefs he concluded that whoever difpleafed Henry VIII. was of courfe put to death.

† This is a miftake; it was the furcoat of Edward IV. enriched with rubies, and was preferved here till the civil war.

strength, and beautified with fine buildings and a Tower; it was an antient castle, of which old annals speak in this manner: king Edward, A. D. 1359, began a new building in that part of the Castle of Windsor where he was born; for which reason he took care it should be decorated with larger and finer edifices than the rest. In this part were kept prisoners John king of France, and David king of Scots, over whom Edward triumphed at one and the same time: it was by their advice, struck with the advantage of its situation, and with the sums paid for their ransom, that by degrees this Castle stretched to such magnificence, as to appear no longer a fortress, but a town of proper extent, and inexpugnable to any human force; this particular part of the Castle was built at the sole expence of the king of Scotland, except one tower, which, from its having been erected by the Bishop of Winchester, Prelate of the Order, is called Winchester Tower*; there are a hundred steps to it, so ingeniously contrived that horses can easily ascend them; it is an hundred and fifty paces in circuit; within it are preserved all manner of arms necessary for the defence of the place.

The third court is much the largest of any, built at the expence of the captive king of France; as it stands higher, so it greatly excels the two former in splendor and elegance; it has one hundred and

---

* This is confounded with the round tower.

forty-eight paces in length, and ninety-seven in breadth; in the middle of it is a fountain of very clear water, brought under ground, at an exceffive expence, from the diftance of four miles. Towards the eaft are magnificent apartments deftined for the royal houfehold; towards the weft is a tennis-court for the amufement of the court; on the north fide are the royal apartments, confifting of magnificent chambers, halls, and bathing-rooms *, and a private chapel, the roof of which is embellifhed with golden rofes and fleurs de lis: in this, too, is that very large banqueting-room, feventy-eight paces long, and thirty wide, in which the Knights of the Garter annually celebrate the memory of their tutelar faint, St. George, with a folemn and moft pompous fervice.

From hence runs a walk of incredible beauty, three hundred and eighty paces in length, fet round on every fide with fupporters of wood, which fuftain a balcony, from whence the nobility and perfons of diftinction can take the pleafure of feeing hunting and hawking in a lawn of fufficient fpace; for the fields and meadows, clad with variety of plants and flowers, fwell gradually into hills of perpetual verdure quite up to the caftle, and at bottom ftretch out in an extended plain, that ftrikes the beholders with delight.

* It is not clear what the author means by *hypocauftis*; I have tranflated it bathing-rooms; it might mean only chambers with ftoves.

Besides what has been already mentioned, there are worthy of notice here two bathing-rooms, cieled and wainscoted with looking-glass; the chamber in which Henry VI. was born; queen Elizabeth's bed-chamber, where is a table of red marble with white streaks; a gallery every where ornamented with emblems and figures; a chamber in which are the royal beds of Henry VII. and his queen, of Edward VI., of Henry VIII., and of Anne Bullen, all of them eleven feet square, and covered with quilts shining with gold and silver; queen Elizabeth's bed, with curious coverings of embroidery, but not quite so long or large as the others; a piece of tapestry, in which is represented Clovis, king of France, with an angel presenting to him the fleurs de lis, to be born in his arms; for before his time the kings of France bore three toads in their shield, instead of which they afterwards placed three fleurs de lis on a blue field; this antique tapestry is said to have been taken from a king of France, while the English were masters there. We were shewn here, among other things, the horn of a unicorn, of above eight spans and a half in length, valued at above 10,000l.; the bird of paradise, three spans long, three fingers broad, having a blue bill of the length of half an inch, the upper part of its head yellow, the nether part of a * * * * colour*; a little lower from either side of its throat stick out

---

* The original is *optici;* it is impossible to guess what colour he meant.

some redish feathers, as well as from its back and the rest of its body; its wings of a yellow colour are twice as long as the bird itself; from its back grow out lengthways two fibres or nerves, bigger at their ends, but like a pretty strong thread, of a leaden colour, inclining to black, with which, as it has no feet, it is said to fasten itself to trees, when it wants to rest; a cushion most curiously wrought by queen Elizabeth's own hands.

In the precincts of Windsor, on the other side the Thames, both whose banks are joined by a bridge of wood, is ETON, a well-built College, and famous school for polite letters, founded by Henry VI.; where, besides a master, eight fellows and chanters, sixty boys are maintained gratis. They are taught grammar, and remain in the school till, upon trial made of their genius and progress in study, they are sent to the University of Cambridge.

As we were returning to our inn, we happened to meet some country people *celebrating their harvest-home;* their last load of corn they crown with flowers, having besides an image richly dressed, by which, perhaps, they would signify Ceres; this they keep moving about, while men and women, men and maid servants, riding through the streets in the cart, shout as loud as they can till they arrive at the barn. The farmers here do not bind up their corn in sheaves, as they do with us, but directly they have reaped or mowed it, put it into carts, and convey it into their barns.

We went through the town of Staines.

Hampton-Court, a royal palace, magnificently built with brick by Cardinal Wolfey in oftentation of his wealth, where he enclofed five very ample courts, confifting of noble edifices in very beautiful work. Over the gate in the fecond area is the queen's device, a golden Rofe, with this motto, DIEU ET MON DROIT: on the inward fide of this gate are the effigies of the twelve Roman emperors in plaifter. The chief area is paved with fquare ftone; in its center is a fountain that throws up water, covered with a gilt crown, on the top of which is a ftatue of Juftice, fupported by columns of black and white marble. The chapel of this palace is moft fplendid, in which the queen's clofet is quite tranfparent, having its window of chryftal. We were led into two chambers, called the prefence, or chambers of audience, which fhone with tapeftry of gold and filver and filk of different colours: under the canopy of ftate are thefe words embroidered in pearl, *Vivat Henricus Octavus*. Here is befides a fmall chapel richly hung with tapeftry, where the queen performs her devotions. In her bed-chamber the bed was covered with very coftly coverlids of filk: at no great diftance from this room we were fhewn a bed, the teafter of which was worked by Anne Bullen, and prefented by her to her hufband Henry VIII. All the other rooms, being very numerous, are adorned with tapeftry of gold, filver, and velvet, in fome of which were woven hiftory pieces; in others, Turkifh and American dreffes, all extremely natural.

In the hall are thefe curiofities:

A very clear looking-glafs, ornamented with columns and little images of alabafter; a portrait of Edward VI., brother to queen Elizabeth; the true portrait of Lucretia; a picture of the battle of Pavia; the hiftory of Chrift's paffion, carved in mother of pearl; the portraits of Mary queen of Scots, who was beheaded, and her daughter *; the picture of Ferdinand prince of Spain, and of Philip his fon; that of Henry VIII., under it was placed the Bible curioufly written upon parchment; an artificial fphere; feveral mufical inftruments; in the tapeftry are reprefented negroes riding upon elephants. The bed in which Edward VI. is faid to have been born, and where his mother Jane Seymour died in child-bed; in one chamber were feveral exceffively rich tapeftries, which are hung up when the queen gives audience to foreign ambaffadors; there were numbers of cufhions ornamented with gold and filver; many counterpanes and coverlids of beds lined with ermine: in fhort, all the walls

* Here are feveral miftakes.

of the palace shine with gold and silver. Here is besides a certain cabinet called Paradise, where besides that every thing glitters so with silver, gold, and jewels, as to dazzle one's eyes, there is a musical instrument made all of glass, except the strings. Afterwards we were led into the gardens, which are most pleasant; here we saw rosemary so planted and nailed to the walls as to cover them entirely, which is a method exceeding common in England.

Kingston, a market town.

Nonesuch, a royal retreat, in a place formerly called Cuddington, a very healthful situation, chosen by king Henry VIII. for his pleasure and retirement, and built by him with an excess of magnificence and elegance, even to ostentation: one would imagine every thing that architecture can perform to have been employed in this one work. There are every where so many statues that seem to breathe so many miracles of consummate art, so many casts that rival even the perfection of Roman antiquity, that it may well claim and justify its name of Nonesuch, being without an equal; or as the poet sung,

This, which no equal has in art or fame,
Britons deservedly do *Nonesuch* name.

The palace itself is so encompassed with parks full of deer, delicious gardens, groves ornamented with trellis work, cabinets of verdure, and walks

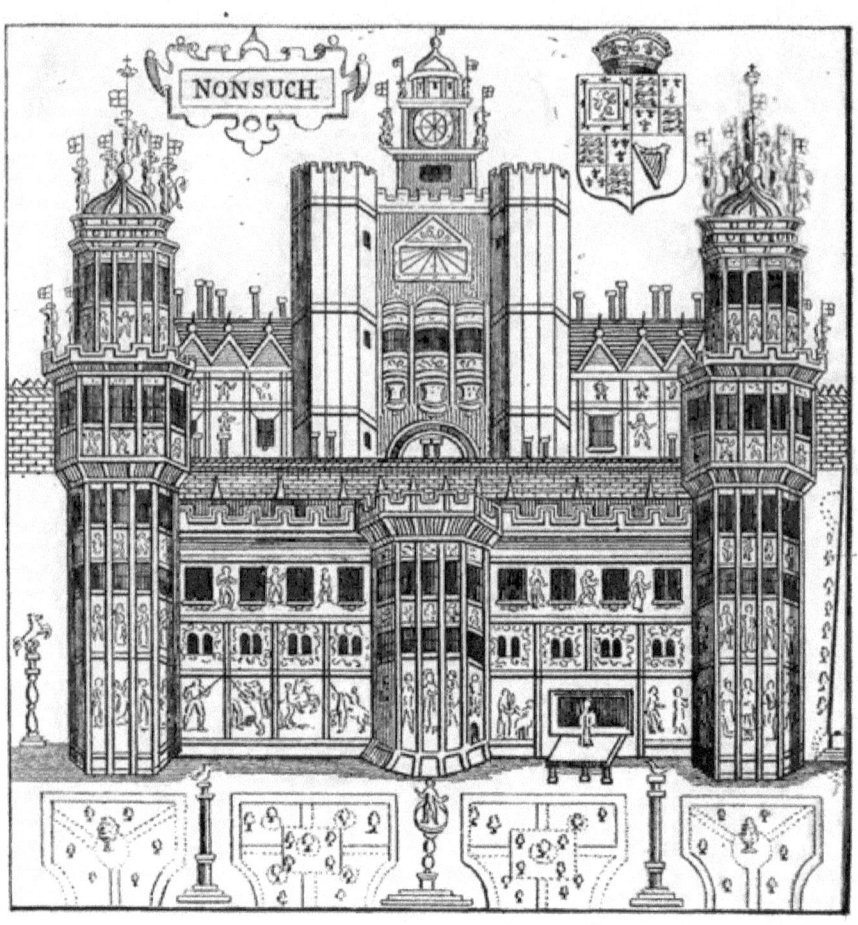

so embrowned by trees, that it seems to be a place pitched upon by *Pleasure* herself, to dwell in along with *Health*.

In the pleasure and artificial gardens are many columns and pyramids of marble, two fountains that spout water one round the other like a pyramid, upon which are perched small birds that stream water out of their bills. In the grove of Diana is a very agreeable fountain, with Actæon turned into a stag, as he was sprinkled by the goddess and her nymphs, with inscriptions.

There is besides another pyramid of marble full of concealed pipes, which spirt upon all who come within their reach.

Returned from hence to London.

A

SHORT DESCRIPTION

OF

ENGLAND.

BRITAIN, confifting of the two kingdoms of England and Scotland, is the largeft ifland in the world, encompaffed by the ocean, the German and French feas. The largeft and fouthern part of it is England, fo named from the Angli, who quitting the little territory yet called Angel in the kingdom of Denmark, took poffeffion here. It is governed by its own king, who owns no fuperior but God. It is divided into thirty-nine counties, to which thirteen in Wales were added by Henry VIII., the firft who diftributed that principality into counties; over each of thefe, in times of danger, a lord lieutenant, nominated by the king, prefides with an unlimited power. Every year fome gentleman, an inhabitant of the place, is appointed fheriff; his office is to collect the public monies, to raife fines, or to make feizures, and account for it to the treafury; to attend upon the judges, and put their fentence in execution; to empannel the jury, who fit upon facts, and return their verdict to the judges, (who in England are only fuch of the law, and not of the fact); to convey the condemned to execution, and to determine in leffer caufes, for the greater are tried by the judges, formerly called travelling judges, now judges of affize; thefe go their circuits through the counties twice every year to hear caufes, and pronounce fentence upon prifoners.

As to ecclefiaftical jurifdiction, after the popes had affigned a church and parifh to every prieft, Honorius, archbifhop of Canterbury, about the year 636, began to divide England in the fame manner into parifhes: as it has two provinces, fo it has two archbifhops; the one of Canterbury, primate and metropolitan of all England; the other of York: fubject to thefe are twenty-five bifhops, viz. twenty-two to Canterbury, the remaining three to York.

The foil is fruitful, and abounds with cattle, which inclines the inhabitants rather to feeding than ploughing, fo that near a third part of the land is left uncultivated for grazing. The climate is moft temperate at all times, and the air never heavy, confequently maladies are fcarcer, and lefs phyfic is ufed there than any where elfe. There are but few rivers: though the foil is productive, it bears no wine; but that want is fupplied from abroad by the beft kinds, as of Orleans, Gafcon, Rhenifh, and Spanifh. The general drink is beer, which is prepared from barley, and is excellently well tafted, but ftrong, and what foon fuddles. There are many hills without one tree, or any spring, which produce a very short and tender grafs, and supply plenty of food to sheep; upon these wander numerous flocks, extremely white, and whether from the temperature of the air, or goodnefs of the earth, bearing softer and finer fleeces than those of any other country: this is the true Golden Fleece, in which confift the chief riches of the inhabitants, great sums of money being brought into the ifland by merchants, chiefly for that article of trade. The dogs here are particularly good. It has mines of gold, silver, and tin, (of which all manner of table utenfils are made, in brightnefs equal to silver, and used all over Europe), of lead, and of iron, but not much of the latter. The horfes are small but swift. Glaff-houfes are in plenty here.

Of the Manners of the English.

The Englifh are ferious, like the Germans; lovers of fhew, liking to be followed wherever they go by whole troops of fervants, who wear their mafters' arms in silver, faftened to their left arms, a ridicule they defervedly lay under. They excel in dancing and mufic, for they are active and lively, though of a thicker make than the French; they cut their hair clofe on the middle of the head, letting it grow on either fide; they are good failors, and better pirates, cunning, treacherous, and thievifh; above three hundred are faid to be hanged annually at London; beheading with them is lefs infamous than hanging; they give the wall as the place of honour; hawking is the general fport of the gentry; they are more polite in eating than the French, devouring lefs bread, but more meat, which they roaft in perfection; they put a great deal of fugar in their drink; their beds are covered with tapeftry, even thofe of farmers; they are often molefted with the fcurvy, faid to have firft crept into England with the Norman conqueft; their houfes are commonly of two ftories, except in London, where they are of three and four, though but feldom of four; they are built of wood, thofe of the richer fort with bricks; their roofs are low, and, where the owner has money, covered with lead.

They are powerful in the field, fuccefsful againft their enemies, impatient of any thing like flavery; vaftly fond of great noifes that fill the ear, fuch as the firing of cannon, drums, and the ringing of bells, fo that it is common for a number of them, that have got a glafs in their heads, to go up into fome belfrey, and ring the bells for hours together for the fake of exercife. If they fee a foreigner very well made, or particularly handfome, they will fay, *It is a pity he is not an* Englifhman!

The Illustrious

FAMILIES of ENGLAND.

* THOMAS Howard †, duke of Norfolk, hereditary marshal of England: the dutchy is extinct for rebellion, the last duke being beheaded.

Grey †, duke of Suffolk, attainted under queen Mary.

Philip Howard, earl of Arundel in his mother's right, and of Surry by his father, son of the above-mentioned duke of Norfolk, he himself condemned for high treason, and his titles forfeited.

Edward Vere, earl of Oxford, hereditary chamberlain of England.

Percy, earl of Northumberland, descended from the dukes of Brabant.

Charles Nevill †, earl of Westmoreland, banished into Holland, and deprived of his fortunes and dignities for rebellion.

* Those marked with a † are extinct, or forfeited.

Talbot, earl of Shrewſbury.

Grey, earl of Kent, has but a ſmall eſtate.

Stanley, earl of Derby, and king of Man.

Manners, earl of Rutland.

Somerſet, earl of Worceſter, deſcended from a baſtard of the Somerſet family, which itſelf is of the royal family of the Plantagenets.

Clifford, earl of Cumberland.

Ratcliff, earl of Suſſex.

Haſtings, earl of Huntingdon, of the line of York, by the mother's ſide.

Bourchier, earl of Bath.

Ambroſe Sutton †, alias Dudley, earl of Warwick, died a few years ſince childleſs.

Wriotheſly, earl of Southampton.

Ruſſel, earl of Bedford.

Herbert, earl of Pembroke.

Edward Seymour †, earl of Hertford, ſon of the

HENRY WRIOTHESLY.
3ᵈ Earl of Southampton.
Ob. Novʳ. 10ᵗʰ 1624.

Charles Howard,
Earl of Nottingham,
Lord High Admiral.
Knight of the Garter &c.
born 1536   died 1624.
Publish'd May 20th 1797 by E. Jeffery Pall Mall.

duke of Somerset, who was beheaded in the reign of Edward VI.

Robert Sutton †, or Dudley, earl of Leicester, brother of the earl of Warwick, died a few years ago.

Robert d'Evereux, earl of Essex, and of Ewe in Normandy, created hereditary marshal of England, in 1598.

Charles Howard, of the Norfolk family, created earl of Nottingham 1597, lord high admiral of England, and privy counsellor.

Fiesnes, earl of Lincoln.

Brown, viscount Montacute.

Howard, of the Norfolk family, viscount Bindon.

Nevill, baron Abergavenny: this Barony is controverted.

Touchet, baron Audley.

Zouch, baron Zouch.

Peregrine Bertie, baron Willoughby of Eresby and Brooke, governor of Berwick.

Berkley, baron Berkley, of the antient family of the kings of Denmark.

Parker, baron Morley.

Dacre †, baron Dacre of Gyllefland: this barony is vacant.

Dacre †, baron Dacre of the South: he died four years fince, and the barony devolved to his daughter.

Brook, baron Cobham, warden of the cinque ports.

Stafford, baron Stafford, reduced to want; he is heir to the family of the dukes of Buckingham, who were hereditary conftables of England.

Gray, baron Gray of Wilton.

Scroop, baron Scroop of Boulton.

Sutton, baron Dudley.

Stourton, baron Stourton.

Nevill †, baron Latimer, died fome years fince without heirs male; the title controverted.

Lumley, baron Lumley.

Blunt, baron Montjoy.

Ogle, baron Ogle.

Darcy, baron Darcy.

Parker, baron Montegle, fon and heir of baron Morley; he has this barony in right of his mother, of the family of Stanley.

Sandys, baron Sandys.

Vaux, baron Vaux.

Windfor, baron Windfor.

Wentworth, baron Wentworth.

Borough, baron Borough, reduced to want.

Baron Mordaunt.   Baron Eure.

Baron Rich.   Baron Sheffield.

Baron North, privy counfellor, and treafurer of the houfehold.

Baron Hunfdon, privy counfellor, and lord chamberlain.

Sackville, baron Buckhurft, privy counfellor.

Thom. Cecil, baron Burleigh, fon of the treafurer.

Cecil, Lord Roos, grandson of the treasurer, yet a child: he holds the barony in right of his mother, daughter to the earl of Rutland.

Howard † of Maltravers, son of the earl of Arundel, not yet restored in blood.

Baron Cheyny †.

Baron Cromwell.   Baron Wharton.

Baron Willoughby of Parham.

Baron Pagett †, in exile, attainted.

Baron Chandois.   Baron St. John.

Baron Delaware: his ancestors took the king of France prisoner.

Baron Compton, has squandered almost all his substance.

Baron Norris.

Thomas Howard, second son of the duke of Norfolk, baron Audley of Saffronwalden, in his mother's right.

William †, third son of the duke of Norfolk, is neither a baron, nor yet restored in blood.

Thus far of NOBLE FAMILIES.

We set out from London in a boat, and fell down the river, leaving Greenwich, which we have spoken of before, on the right hand.

Barking, a town in sight on the left.

Gravesend, a small town, famous for the convenience of its port; the largest Dutch ships usually call here. As we were to proceed farther from hence by water, we took our last leave here of the noble Bohemian David Strziela, and his tutor Tobias Salander, our constant fellow-travellers through France and England, they designing to return home through Holland, we on a second tour into France; but it pleased heaven to put a stop to their design, for the worthy Strziela was seized with a diarrhea a few days before our departure, and, as we afterwards learned by letters from Salander, died in a few days of a violent fever in London.

Queenborough: we left the Castle on our right; a little farther we saw the fishing of oysters out of the sea, which are no where in greater plenty or perfection; witness Ortelius in his Epitome, &c.

Whitstable; here we went ashore.

Canterbury; we came to it on foot; this is the seat of the archbishop, primate of all England, a very antient town, and, without doubt, of note in the time of the Romans.

Here are two monasteries almost contiguous, namely of Christ and St. Augustine, both of them once filled with Benedictine Monks: the former was afterwards dedicated to St. Thomas Becket, the name of Christ being obliterated; it stands almost in the middle of the town, and with so much majesty lifts itself, and its two towers, to a stupendous height, that, as Erasmus says, it strikes even those, who only see it at a distance, with awe.

In the choir, which is shut up with iron rails, are the following monuments:

King Henry IV., with his wife Joan of Navarre, of white marble.

Nicholas Wootton, privy counsellor to Henry VIII., Edward VI., Mary, and Elizabeth, kings and queens of England.

Of prince Edward, duke of Aquitain and Cornwall, and earl of Chester.

Reginald Pole, with this inscription:

The remains of Reginald Pole, Cardinal and Archbishop of Canterbury.

Cardinal Chatillon.

We were then shewn the chair in which the bishops are placed when they are installed. In the vestibule of the church, on the south side, stand the statues of three men armed, cut in stone, who slew Thomas Becket, archbishop of Canterbury, made a Saint for this martyrdom; their names are adjoined,

Tusci, Fusci, Berri *.

Being tired with walking, we refreshed ourselves here with a mouthful of bread and some ale, and immediately mounted post-horses, and arrived about two or three o'clock in the morning at Dover. In our way to it, which was rough and dangerous enough, the following accident happened to us: our guide, or postillion, a youth, was before with two of our company, about the distance of a musket-shot; we, by not following quick enough, had lost sight of our friends; we came afterwards to where the road divided; on the right it was down hill and marshy, on the left was a small hill: whilst we stopped here in doubt, and consulted which of the roads we should take, we saw all on a sudden on our right hand some horsemen, their stature, dress, and horses, exactly resembling those of our friends; glad of having found them again, we determined to set on after them; but it happened, through God's mercy, that though we called to them, they did not answer us, but kept on down the marshy

---

* This is another most inaccurate account: the murderers of Becket were *Tracy*, *Morville*, *Britton*, and *Fitzurse*.

road at such a rate, that their horses' feet struck fire at every stretch, which made us, with reason, begin to suspect they were thieves, having had warning of such; or rather, that they were nocturnal spectres, who, as we were afterwards told, are frequently seen in those places: there were, likewise, a great many Jack-w'-a-lanterns, so that we were quite seized with horror and amazement!——But fortunately for us, our guide soon after sounded his horn, and we, following the noise, turned down the left-hand road, and arrived safe to our companions; who, when we had asked them, if they had not seen the horsemen who had gone by us? answered, not a soul. Our opinions, according to custom, were various upon this matter; but whatever the thing was, we were, without doubt, in imminent danger, from which that we escaped, the glory is to be ascribed to God alone.

Dover, situated among cliffs, (standing where the port itself was originally, as may be gathered from anchors and parts of vessels dug up there) is more famous for the convenience of its port, which indeed is now much decayed, and its passage to France, than for either its elegance or populousness: this passage, the most used and the shortest, is of thirty miles, which, with a favourable wind, may be run over in five or six hours time, as we ourselves experienced; some reckon it only eighteen to Calais, and to Boulogne sixteen English miles, which, as Ortelius says in his Theatrum, are longer than the Italian.

Here was a church dedicated to St. Martin by Victred, king of Kent, and a houfe belonging to the Knights Templars; of either there are now no remains. It is the feat of a fuffragan to the archbifhop of Canterbury, who, when the archbifhop is employed upon bufinefs of more confequence, manages the ordinary affairs, but does not interfere with the archiepifcopal jurifdiction. Upon a hill, or rather rock, which on its right fide is almoft every where a precipice, a very extenfive caftle rifes to a furprifing height, in fize like a little city, extremely well fortified, and thick fet with towers, and feems to threaten the fea beneath. Matthew Paris calls it the door and key of England; the ordinary people have taken it into their heads that it was built by Julius Cæfar; it is likely it might by the Romans, from thofe Britifh bricks in the chapel which they made ufe in their foundations. See Cambden's Britannia.

After we had dined, we took leave of ENGLAND.

FRAGMENTA REGALIA:

Or, *Observations on the late Queen Elizabeth, her Times, and Favourites—Written by Sir Robert Naunton, Master of the Court of Wards.* A. D. 1641.

TO take her in the original, she was the daughter of king Henry VIII. by Ann Bullen, the second of six wives which he had, and one of the maids of honour to the divorced queen, Katharine of Austria, (or, as the now stiled, Infanta of Spain) and from thence taken to the royal bed.

That she was of a most noble and royal extract by her father will not fall into question, for on that side was disembogued into her veins, by a confluency of blood, the very abstract of all the greatest houses in Christendom: and remarkable it is, considering that violent desertion of the Royal House of the Britons by the intrusion of the Saxons, and afterwards by the conquest of the Normans, that, through vicissitude of times, and after a discontinuance almost of a thousand years, the scepter should fall again, and be brought back, into the old regal line and true current of the British blood, in the person of her renowned grandfather, king Henry VII., together with whatsoever the German, Norman, Burgundian, Castilian, and French, achievements, with their intermarriages, which eight hundred years had acquired, could add of glory thereunto.

By her mother she was of no sovereign descent, yet noble and very antient in the family of Bullen; though some erroneously brand them with a citizen's rise or original, which was yet but of a second brother, who (as it was divine in the greatness and lustre to come to his house) was sent into the city to acquire wealth, *ad ædificandam antiquam domum*, unto whose achievements (for he was Lord Mayor of London) fell in, as it is averred, both the blood and inheritance of the eldest brother for want of issue males, by which accumulation the house within few descents mounted, *in culmen honoris*, and was suddenly dilated in the best families of England and Ireland; as Howard, Ormond, Sackville, and others.

Having thus touched, and now leaving her stipe, I come to her person, and how she came to the crown by the decease of her brother and sister.

Under Edward VI. she was his, and one of the darlings of Fortune, for, besides the consideration of blood, there was between these two princes a concurrency and sympathy of their natures and affections, together with the celestial bond, (confirmative religion) which made them one; for the king never called her by any other appellation but his sweetest and dearest sister, and was scarce his own man, she being absent; which was not so between him and the lady Mary.

Under her sister* she found her condition much altered; for it was resolved, and her destiny had decreed it, for to set her apprentice in the school of affliction, and to draw her through that Ordeal-fire of trial, the better to mould and fashion her to rule and sovereignty: which finished, Fortune calling to mind that the time of her servitude was expired, gave up her indentures, and therewith delivered into her custody a scepter as the reward of her patience; which was about the twenty-sixth of her age; a time in which, as for her internals grown ripe, and seasoned by adversity, in the exercise of her virtue; for, it seems, Fortune meant no more but to shew her a piece of variety and changeableness of her nature, but to conduct her to her destiny, i. e. felicity.

She was of person tall, of hair and complection fair, and therewith well favoured, but high-nosed; of limbs and features neat; and, which added to the lustre of these external graces, of a stately and

* Queen Mary.

majeftic comportment, participating in this more of her father than of her mother, who was of an inferior alloy, plaufible, or, as the French hath it, more *debonaire* and affable: virtues which might well fuit with majefty, and which, defcending as hereditary to the daughter, did render her of a fweeter temper, and endeared her more to the love and liking of the people, who gave her the name and fame of a moft gracious and popular princefs.

The atrocity of the father's nature was rebated in her by the mother's fweeter inclinations; for (to take, and that no more than the character out of his own mouth) *He never fpared man in his anger, nor woman in his luft.*

If we fearch farther into her intellectuals and abilities, the wheel-courfe of her government deciphers them to the admiration of pofterity; for it was full of magnanimity, tempered with juftice, piety, and pity, and, to fpeak truth, noted but with one act of ftain or taint, all her deprivations, either of life or liberty, being legal and neceffitated. She was learned, her fex and time confidered, beyond common belief; for letters about *this* time, or fomewhat *before*, did but begin to be of efteem and in fafhion, the former ages being overcaft with the mifts and fogs of the Roman * ignorance; and it was the maxim that over-ruled the foregoing times,

* Viz. Popifh.

that *Ignorance was the mother of Devotion*. Her wars were a long time more in the auxiliary part, and affiftance of foreign princes and ftates, than by invafion of any; till common policy advifed it, for a fafer way, to ftrike firft abroad, than at home to expect the war, in all which fhe was ever felicious and victorious.

The change and alteration of religion upon the inftant of her acceffion to the crown (the fmoke and fire of her fifter's martyrdoms fcarcely quenched) was none of her leaft remarkable actions; but the fupport and eftablifhment thereof, with the means of her own fubfiftance amidft fo powerful enemies abroad, and thofe many domeftic practices, were, methinks, works of infpiration, and of no human providence, which, on her fifter's departure, fhe moft religioufly acknowledged, afcribing the glory of her deliverance to God above; for fhe being then at Hatfield, and under a guard, and the parliament fitting at the felf-fame time, at the news of the queen's death, and her own proclamation by the general confent of the houfe and the public fufferance of the people, falling on her knees, after a good time of refpiration, fhe uttered this verfe of the Pfalm:

A Domino factum eft iftud, & eft mirabile in oculis noftris *.

* This is the work of the Lord, and it is wonderful in our fight.

G

And this we find to this day on the stamp of her gold, with this on her silver:

Posui Deum adjutorem meum *.

Her ministers and instruments of state, such as were *participes curarum*, or bore a great part of the burthen, were *many*, and those *memorable;* but they were only *favourites*, and not *minions;* such as acted more by *her* princely rules and judgements, than by their *own* wills and appetites; for we saw no Gaveston, Vere, or Spencer, to have swayed alone, during forty-four years, which was a well-settled and advised maxim; for it valued her the more, it awed the most secure, it took best with the people, and it staved off all emulations, which are apt to rise and vent in obloquious acrimony even against the prince, where there is *one only* admitted into high administrations.

A Major Palatii.

THE principal note of her reign will be, that she ruled much by faction and parties, which she herself both made, upheld, and weakened, as her own great judgement advised; for I do dissent from the common and received opinion, that my lord of Leicester was *absolute* and *alone* in her *grace;* and, though I come somewhat short of the know-

* I have chosen God for my help.

ledge of these times, yet, that I may not err or shoot at random, I know it from assured intelligence that it was not so; for proof whereof, amongst many (that could present) I will both relate a story, and therein a known truth, and it was thus: Bowyer, the gentleman of the Black Rod, being charged by her express command to look precisely to all admissions in the Privy Chamber, one day staid a very gay captain (and a follower of my lord of Leicester) from entrance, for that he was neither well known, nor a sworn servant of the queen; at which repulse, the gentleman (bearing high on my lord's favour) told him, that he might, perchance, procure him a discharge. Leicester coming to the contestation, said publicly, which was none of his wonted speeches, that he was a knave, and should not long continue in his office; and so turning about to go to the queen, Bowyer, who was a bold gentleman and well beloved, stepped before him, and fell at her majesty's feet, relates the story, and humbly craves her grace's pleasure, and in such a manner as if he had demanded, whether my lord of Leicester was king, or her majesty queen: whereunto she replied, (with her wonted oath, *God's-death*) my lord, I have wished you well, but my favour is not so locked up for you, that others shall not participate thereof; for I have many servants unto whom I have, and will, at my pleasure, bequeath my favour, and likewise resume the same; and if you think to rule here, I will take a course to see you forthcoming*; I will have here but one *miſtreſs*, and no *maſter*, and look that no ill happen to him, leſt it be ſeverely required at your hands: which ſo quailed my lord of Leiceſter, that his faint humility was, long after, one of his beſt virtues.

Moreover, the earl of Suſſex, then lord chamberlain, was his profeſſed antagoniſt to his dying day; and for my lord Hunſdown, and ſir Thomas Sackville, after lord treaſurer, who were all contemporaries; he was wont to ſay of them, that they were of the tribe of *Dan*, and were, *Noli me tangere*, implying, that they were not to be conteſted with, for they were, indeed, of the queen's nigh kindred.

From whence, and in many more inſtances, I conclude, that ſhe was abſolute and ſovereign miſtreſs of her graces, and that all thoſe to whom ſhe diſtributed her favours, were never more than tenants at will, and ſtood on no better terms than her princely pleaſure, and their good behaviour.

And this alſo I preſent as a known obſervation, that ſhe was, though very capable of counſel, abſolute enough in her own reſolution; which was ever apparent even to her laſt, and in that of her ſtill averſion to grant Tyrone † the leaſt drop of her mercy, though earneſtly and frequently adviſed

---

* *i. e.* I will confine you.
† The Iriſh rebel.

thereunto, yea, wrought only by her whole council of state, with very many reasons; and, as the state of her kingdom then stood, I may speak it with assurance, necessitated arguments.

If we look into her inclination, as it was disposed to magnificence or frugality, we shall find in them many notable considerations; for all her dispensations were so poised, as though Discretion and Justice had both decreed to stand at the beam, and see them weighed out in due proportion, the maturity of her paces and judgements meeting in a concurrence; and that in such an age that seldom lapseth to excess.

To consider them apart, we have not many precedents of her *liberality*, nor any large donatives to *particular* men, my lord of Essex's book of *parks* excepted, which was a princely gift; and some more of a lesser size to my lord of Leicester, Hatton, and others.

Her rewards chiefly consisted in grants and leases of offices, and places of judicature; but for ready money, and in great sums, she was very sparing; which, we may partly conceive, was a virtue rather drawn out of necessity than her nature; for she had many layings-out, and as her wars were lasting, so their charge increased to the last period. And I am of opinion with sir Walter Rawleigh, that those many brave men of her times, and of the militia, tafted little more of her bounty, than in her grace and good word with their due entertainment; for she ever paid her foldiers well, which was the honour of her times, and more than her great adverfary of Spain could perform; fo that, when we come to the confideration of her *frugality*, the obfervation will be little more, than that her *bounty* and it were fo woven together, that the one was* ftained by an honourable way of fparing.

The Irifh action we may call a malady, and a confumption of her times, for it accompanied her to her end; and it was of fo profufe and vaft an expence, that it drew near unto a diftemperature of ftate, and of paffion in herfelf; for, towards her laft, fhe grew fomewhat hard to pleafe, her armies being accuftomed to profperity, and the Irifh profecution not anfwering her expectation, and her wonted fuccefs; for it was a good while an unthrifty and inaufpicious war, which did much difturb and miflead her judgement; and the more, for that it was a precedent taken out of her own pattern.

For as the queen, by way of divifion, had, at her coming to the crown, fupported the revolted States of Holland, fo did the king of Spain turn the trick upon herfelf, towards her going out, by cherifhing the Irifh rebellion; where it falls into confideration,

* *al.* not

what the state of this kingdom, and the crown revenues, were then able to endure and embrace.

If we look into the establishments of those times with the best of the Irish army, counting the defeatures of Blackwater, with all the precedent expences, as it stood from my lord of Essex's undertaking of the surrender of Kingsale, and the general Mountjoy, and somewhat after, we shall find the horse and foot troops were, for three or four years together, much about twenty thousand, besides the naval charge, which was a dependant of the same war; in that the queen was then forced to keep in continual pay a strong fleet at sea to attend the Spanish coasts and parts, both to alarm the Spaniards, and to intercept the forces designed for the Irish assistance; so that the charge of that war alone did cost the queen three hundred thousand pounds per annum, at least, which was not the moiety of her other disbursements and expences; which, without the public aids, the state of the royal receipts could not have much longer endured; which, out of her own frequent letters and complaints to the deputy Mountjoy for cashiering of that list as soon as he could, might be collected, for the queen was then driven into a strait.

We are naturally prone to applaud the times behind us, and to vilify the present; for the concurrent of her fame carries it to this day, how loyally and victoriously she lived and died, without the grudge and grievance of her people; yet the truth may appear, without retraction, from the honour of so great a princess. It is manifest she left more debts unpaid, taken upon credit of her privy-seals, than her progenitors did, or could have taken up, that were an hundred years before her; which was no inferior piece of state, to lay the burthen on that house*, which was best able to bear it at a dead lift, when neither her receipts could yield her relief at the pinch, nor the urgency of her affairs endure the delays of parliamentary assistance. And for such aids, it is likewise apparent, that she received more, and that with the love of her people, than any two of her predecessors that took most; which was a fortune strained out of the subjects, through the plausibility of her comportment, and (as I would say, without offence) the prodigal distribution of her grace to all sorts of subjects; for I believe no prince living, that was so tender of honour, and so exactly stood for the preservation of sovereignty, was so great a courtier of the people, yea, of the commons, and that stooped and declined low in presenting her person to the public view, as she passed in her progress and perambulations, and in her ejaculations of her prayers on the people.

And, truly, though much may be written in praise of her providence and good husbandry, in that she could, upon all good occasions, abate her magna-

* *al.* Horse.

nimity, and therewith comply with the parliament, and so always come off both with honour and profit; yet must we ascribe some part of the commendation to the wisdom of the times, and the choice of parliament-men; for I said * not that they were at any time given to any violent or pertinacious dispute, the elections being made of grave and discreet persons, not factious and ambitious of fame; such as came not to the house with a malevolent spirit of contention, but with a preparation to consult on the public good, and rather to comply than to contest with majesty: neither dare I find †, that the house was weakened and pestered, through the admission of too many *young heads*, as it hath been of *latter* times; which remembers me of the recorder Martin's speech, about the truth of our late sovereign lord king James ‡, when there were accounts taken of *forty* gentlemen not above *twenty*, and some not exceeding *sixteen* years of age; which made him to say, That it was the antient custom for old men to make laws for young ones, but there he saw the case altered, and that there were children in the great council of the kingdom, which came to invade and invert nature, and to enact laws to govern their fathers. Such § were in the house always ‖, and took the common cause into consideration; and they say the queen had many times just cause, and need enough, to use their assistance: neither do I

* *al.* find.   † *al.* say.   ‡ The First.
§ Fathers.   ‖ During queen Elizabeth's reign.

remember that the house did ever capitulate, or prefer their private to the public and the queen's necessities, but waited their times, and, in the first place, gave their supply, and according to the exigence of her affairs; yet failed not at the last to attain what they desired, so that the queen and her parliaments had ever the good fortunes to depart in love, and on reciprocal terms, which are considerations that have not been so exactly observed in our *last* assemblies. And I would to God they had been; for, considering the great debts left on the king*, and to what incumbrances the house itself had then drawn him, his majesty was not well used, though I lay not the blame on the whole suffrage of the house, where he had many good friends; for I dare avouch it, had the house been freed of half a dozen popular and discontented persons, (such as, with the fellow that burnt the temple of Ephesus, would be talked of, though for doing mischief) I am confident the king had obtained that which, in reason, and at his first occasion, he ought to have received freely, and without condition. But pardon this digression, which is here remembered, not in the way of aggravation, but in true zeal of the public good, and presented in caveat of future times : for I am not ignorant how the genius and spirit of the kingdom now moves to make his majesty amends on any occasion ; and how desirous the subject is to expiate that offence at any rate, may it please his

* Charles the First.

majesty to make a trial of his subjects' affections; and at what price they value now his goodness and magnanimity.

But to our purpose: the queen was not to learn that, as the strength of the kingdom consisted in the multitude of her subjects, so the security of her person consisted and rested in the love and fidelity of her people, which she politically affects (as it hath been thought) somewhat beneath the height of her natural spirit and magnanimity.

Moreover, it will be a true note of her providence, that she would always listen to her profit: for she would not refuse the information of meanest personages, which proposed improvement; and had learned the philosophy of *(hoc agere)* to look unto her own work: of which there is a notable example of one Carmarthen, an under officer of the Custom-House; who, observing his time, presented her with a paper, shewing how she was abused in the under-renting of the customs, and therewith humbly desired her majesty to conceal him, for that it did concern two or three of her great counsellors [*], whom customer Smith had bribed with two thousand pounds a man, so to lose the queen twenty thousand pounds per annum; which being made known to the lords, they gave strict order that Carmarthen should not have access to the back-stairs; but, at

[*] Burleigh, Leicester, and Walsingham.

last, her majesty smelling the craft, and missing Carmarthen, she sent for him back, and encouraged him to stand to his information; which the poor man did so handsomely, that, within the space of ten years, he was brought to double his rent, or leave the Custom to new farmers. So that we may take this also in confideration, that there were of the queen's council, which were not in the catalogue of faints.

Now, as we have taken a view of some particular motives of her times, her nature, and necessities, it is not without the text to give a short touch of the *helps* and *advantages* of her reign, which were *not* without[*] paroles; for she had neither husband, brother, sister, nor children, to provide for, who, as they are dependants on the crown, so do they necessarily draw livelihood from thence, and oftentimes exhaust and draw deep, especially when there is an ample fraternity royal, and of the princes of the blood, as it was in the time of Edward III., and Henry IV. For when the crown cannot, the public ought to give honourable allowance; for they are the honour and hopes of the kingdom; and the public, which enjoys them, hath the like interest with the father which begat them; and our common law, which is the inheritance of the kingdom, did ever, of old, provide aids for the *primogenitus* [†] and the eldest daughter; for that the multiplicity of

---

[*] *al.* were without.   [†] The eldest son.

courts, and the great charges which neceffarily follow
a king, a queen, a prince, and royal iffue, was a thing
which was not *in rerum natura* *, during the fpace
of forty-four years †, but worn out of memory, and
without the confideration of the prefent times, infomuch as the aids given to the late and right noble
prince Henry, and to his fifter, the lady Elizabeth,
which were at firft generally received as impofitions
for knighthood, though an antient law, fell alfo into
the imputation of a tax of nobility, for that it lay
long covered in the embers of divifion between the
houfes of York and Lancafter, and forgotten or
connived at by the fucceeding princes: fo that the
ftrangenefs of the obfervation, and the difference of
thofe latter reigns, is, that the queen took up much
beyond the power of law, which fell not into the
murmur of people; and her fucceffors took nothing
but by warrant of the law, which, neverthelefs,
was received, *through difufe*, to be injurious to the
liberty of the kingdom.

Now before I come to any mention of her favourites, for hitherto I have delivered but fome ob-
livious paffages, thereby to prepare and fmooth a
way for the reft that follows:

It is neceffary that I touch on the religioufnefs of
the other's reign, I mean the body of her fifter's ‡

* Exifting.
† Which fhe ruled the Englifh fcepter.   ‡ Mary.

council of state, which she retained entirely, neither removing nor discontenting any, although she knew them averse to her religion, and, in her sister's time, perverse to her person, and privy to all her troubles and imprisonments.

A prudence which was incompatible to her sister's nature, for she both dissipated and presented the major part of her brother's council; but this will be of certain, that how compliable and obsequious soever she found them, yet for a good space she made little use of their counsels, more than in the ordinary course of the board, for she had a dormant table in her own privy breast; yet she kept them together, and in their places, without any sudden change; so that we may say of them, that they were then of the court, not of the council; for whilst she *amazed* * them by a kind of promissive disputation, concerning the points controverted by both churches, she did set down her own gests, without their privity, and made all their progressions, gradations; but for that the tenents of her secrets, with the intents of her establishments, were pitched before it was known where the court would sit down.

Neither do I find that any of her sister's council of state were either repugnant to her religion, or opposed her doings; Englefeild, master of the

* *al.* amused.

wards, excepted, who withdrew himself from the board, and shortly after out of her dominions; so pliable and obedient they were to change with the times and their prince; and of them will fall a relation of recreation. Pawlet, marquis of Winchester, and lord treasurer, had served then four princes, in as various and changeable times and seasons, that I may well say no time nor age hath yielded the like precedent: this man being noted to grow high in her favour, (as his place and experience required) was questioned by an intimate friend of his, how he had stood up for thirty years together, amidst the change and ruins of so many chancellors and great personages: why, quoth the marquis, *Ortus sum e salice, non ex quercu*, i.e. *I am made of pliable willow, not of the stubborn oak.* And, truly, it seems the old man had taught them all, especially William earl of Pembroke, for they two were always of the king's religion, and always zealous professors: of these it is said, that being both younger brothers, yet of noble houses, they spent what was left them, and came on trust to the court, where, upon the bare stock of their wits, they began to traffic for themselves, and prospered so well, that they got, spent, and left, more than any subjects from the Normans conquest to their own times; whereupon it hath been prettily spoken, that they lived in a time of dissolution.

To conclude, then, of all the former reign, it is said, that those two lived and died chiefly in her grace and favour: by the letter written upon his son's marriage with the lady Catherine Grey, he had like utterly to have loft himself; but at the inftant of confummation, as apprehending the unfafety and danger of intermarriage with the blood royal, he fell at the queen's feet, where he both acknowledged his prefumption, and projected the caufe and the divorce together: fo quick he was at his work, that in the time of repudiation of the faid lady Grey, he clapped up a marriage for his fon, the lord Herbert, with Mary Sidney, daughter to fir Henry Sidney, then lord deputy of Ireland, the blow falling on Edward, the late earl of Hertford, who, to his coft, took up the divorced lady, of whom the lord Beauchamp was born, and William, now earl of Hertford, is defcended.

I come now to prefent them to her own election, which were either admitted to her fecrets of ftate, or took into her grace and favour; of whom, in order, I crave leave to give unto pofterity a cautious defcription, with a fhort character or draught of the perfons themfelves; for, without offence to others, I would be true to myfelf, their memories and merits, diftinguifhing thofe of *Militiæ* * from the *Togati* †; and of both thefe fhe had as many, and thofe as able minifters, as had any of her progenitors.

* Camp. † Council.

Robert Earl of Leicester

From an Original Drawing by Zuccaro in the Possession of Lord Frederick Campbell

Pub.d Jan.y 1 1747 by T Jefferys

LEICESTER.

IT will be out of doubt, that my lord of Leicester was one of the first whom she made master of the horse; he was the youngest son then living of the duke of Northumberland, beheaded *primo Mariæ* *, and his father was that Dudley which our histories couple with Empson; and both be much infamed for the caterpillars of the commonwealth, during the reign of Henry the Seventh, who, being of a noble extract, was executed the first year of Henry the Eighth, but not thereby so extinct, but that he left a plentiful estate, and such a son, who, as the vulgar speaks it, would live without a teat; for, out of the ashes of his father's infamy, he rose to be a duke, and as high as subjection could permit, or sovereignty endure; and though he could not find out any appellation to assume the crown in his own person, yet he projected, and very nearly effected it, for his son Gilbert, by intermarriage with the lady Jane Grey, and so, by that way, to bring it into his loins.

Observations which, though they lie beyond us, and seem impertinent to the text, yet are they not much extravagant, for they must lead us, and shew us how the after-passages were brought about, with

* In the first year of queen Mary.

the dependances on the line of a collateral workmanship; and surely it may amaze a well-settled judgement to look back into these times, and to consider how the duke could attain to such a pitch of greatness, his father dying in ignominy, and at the gallows, his estate confiscated for pilling and polling the people.

But, when we better think upon it, we find that he was given up, but as a sacrifice to please the people, not for any offence committed against the person of the king; so that upon the matter he was a martyr of the prerogative, and the king in honour could do no less than give back to his son the privilege of his blood, with the acquiring of his father's profession, for he was a lawyer, and of the king's council, at law, before he came to be *ex interioribus consiliis* *, where, besides the licking of his own fingers, he got the king a mass of riches, and that not with hazard, but with the loss of his life and fame, for the king's father's sake.

Certain it is, that his son was left rich in purse and brain; which are good foundations, and fewel to ambition; and, it may be supposed, he was on all occasions well heard of the king, as a person of mark and compassion in his eye, but I find not that he did put up for advancement, during Henry the Eighth's time, although a vast aspirer, and a provident stayer.

* Of his privy-council.

It feems, he thought the king's reign was much given to the falling-ficknefs, but efpying his time fitting, and the fovereignty in the hands of a pupil prince, he then thought he might as well put up, for it was the beft ; for having the poffeffion of blood, and of purfe, with a head-piece of a vaft extent, he foon got to honour, and no fooner there, but he began to fide it with the beft, even with the protector *, and, in conclufion, got his and his brother's heads; ftill afpiring, till he expired in the lofs of his own ; fo that pofterity may by reading of the father, and grandfather, make judgement of the fon ; for we fhall find that this Robert, whofe original we have now traced, the better to prefent him, was inheritor to the genius and craft of his father; and Ambrofe, of the eftate, of whom hereafter we fhall make fome fhort mention.

We took him now as he was admitted into the court and the queen's favours, and here he was not to feek to play his part well and dexteroufly ; but his play was chiefly at the fore-game, not that he was a learner at the latter, but he loved not the after-wit, for the report is, (and I think not unjuftly) that he was feldom behind-hand with his gamefters, and that they always went with the lofs.

He was a very goodly perfon, tall, and fingularly well featured, and all his youth well favoured, of a

* The duke of Somerfet.

sweet aspect, but high foreheaded, which (as I should take it) was of no discommendation; but, towards his latter, and which with old men was but a middle age, he grew high coloured; so that the queen had much of her father, for, excepting some of her kindred, and some few that had handsome wits in crooked bodies, she always took personage in the way of election, for the people hath it to this day, *king Henry loved a man.*

Being thus in her grace, she called to mind the sufferings of *his* ancestors, both in her father's and sister's reigns, and restored his and his brother's blood, creating Ambrose, the elder, earl of Warwick, and himself earl of Leicester; and as he was *ex primitis,* or, *of her first choice;* so he rested not there, but long enjoyed her favour, and therewith what he listed, till time and emulation, the companions of greatness, resolved of his period, and to colour him at his setting in a cloud (at Conebury) not by so violent a death, or by the fatal sentence of a judicature, as that of his father and grandfather's was, but, as is supposed, by that poison which he had prepared for others, wherein they report him a rare artist.

I am not bound to give credit to all vulgar relations, or the libels of his time, which are commonly forced and falsified suitable to the words and * ho-

* *al.* Humours.

nours of men in paffion, and difcontent; but what binds me to think him no good man, amongft other things of known truth, is that of my lord of Effex's* death, in Ireland, and the marriage of his lady; which I forbear to prefs, in regard he is long fince dead, and others are living whom it may concern.

To take him in the obfervation of his letters and writings, which fhould beft fet him off, for fuch as have fallen into my hands, I never yet faw a ftile or phrafe more feemingly religious, and fuller of the ftrains of devotion; and, were they not fincere, I doubt much of his well-being †, and, I fear, he was too well feen in the aphorifms and principles of Nicholas the Florentine, and in the reaches ‡ of Cæfar Borgias.

And hereto I have only touched him in his courtfhips. I conclude him in his lance ‖; he was fent governor by the queen to the revolted ftates of Holland, where we read not of his wonders, for they fay, he had more of Mercury, than he had of Mars, and that his device might have been without prejudice to the great Cæfar, *Veni, vidi, redivi.*

* Of which you have an account hereafter in this fmall pamphlet.

† In a future ftate.

‡ The art of poifoning.

‖ Martial ftate.

RADCLIFFE, *Earl of Suffex*.

HIS * co-rival was Thomas Radcliffe, earl of Suffex, who in his conftellation was his direct oppofite, for indeed he was one of the queen's martialifts, and did her very good fervice in Ireland, at her firft acceffion, till fhe recalled him to the court, whom fhe made lord Chamberlain; but he played not his game with that cunning and dexterity, as the earl of Leicefter did, who was much the fairer courtier, though Suffex was thought much the honefter man, and far the better foldier, but he lay too open on his guard; he was a godly gentleman, and of a brave and noble nature, true and conftant to his friends and fervants; he was alfo of a very antient and noble lineage, honoured through many defcents, through the title of Fitzwalters. Moreover, there was fuch an antipathy in his nature to that of Leicefter, that, being together in court, and both in high employments, they grew to a direct frowardnefs, and were in continual oppofition, the one fetting the watch, the other the guard, each on the other's actions and motions; for my lord of Suffex was of fo great fpirit, which, backed with the queen's fpecial favour, and fupport †, by a great and antient inheritance, could not brook the other's empire, infomuch as the queen, upon fundry occa-

---

* Leicefter's.   † *al.* Supported by.

W.m Paulet. 1.st Marquis of Winchester.
Servant to Henry 7.th & for 30 Years Treasurer to Henry 8.th
Edw.d 6.th Queen Mary & Queen Elizabeth. Obit 1572. Æt. 97.
From an Ancient Painting in Kings College, Cambridge.

fions, had fomewhat to do to appeafe and atone them, until death parted the competition, and left the place to Leicefter, who was not long alone, without his rival in grace and command: and to conclude this favourite, it is confidently affirmed, that, lying in his laft ficknefs, he gave this caveat to his friends:

I am now paffing into another world, and I muft leave you to your fortunes, and the queen's grace and goodnefs; but beware of the gipfy, meaning Leicefter, *for he will be too hard for you all; you know not the beaft fo well as I do.*

Secretary WILLIAM CECILL.

I COME now to the next, which was fecretary William Cecill, for, on the death of the old marquis of Winchefter, he came up in his room; a perfon of a moft fubtle and active fpirit.

He ftood not by the way of conftellation, but was wholly attentive to the fervice of his miftrefs, and his dexterity, experience, and merit therein challenged a room in the queen's favour, which eclipfed the others over-feeming greatnefs, and made it appear that there were others fteered and ftood at the helm befides himfelf, and more ftars in the firmament of grace, than Urfa Major.

He was born, as they say, in Lincolnshire, but, as some aver upon knowledge, of a younger brother of the Cecills of Hertfordshire, a family of my own knowledge, though now private, yet of no mean antiquity; who, being exposed, and sent to the city, as poor gentlemen used to do their sons, became to be a rich man on London Bridge, and purchased* in Lincolnshire, where this man was born.

He was sent to Cambridge, and then to the inns of court, and so came to serve the duke of Somerset, in the time of his protectorship † as secretary, and having a pregnancy to high inclinations, he came by degrees to a higher conversation, with the chiefest affairs of State and councils; but, on the fall of the duke, he stood some years in umbrage, and without employment, till the State found they needed his abilities; and although we find not that he was taken into any place, during Mary's reign, unless (as some say) towards the last, yet the council several times made use of him, and in the queen's ‡ entrance he was admitted secretary of State; afterwards he was made master of the Court of Wards, then lord treasurer, for he was a person of most excellent abilities; and indeed the queen began to need and seek out men of both guards, and so I conclude to rank this ‖ great instrument amongst the Togati;

* An estate.   † Under Edward VI.

‡ Elizabeth's.   ‖ Counsellors.

for he had not to do with the sword, more than as the great pay-master, and contriver of the war, which shortly followed, wherein he accomplished much, through his theoretical knowledge at home, and his intelligence abroad, by unlocking of the councils of the queen's enemies.

We must now take it, and that of truth, into observation, that, until the tenth of her reign, the times were calm and serene, though sometimes overcast, as the most glorious sun-rising is subject to shadowings and droppings; for the clouds of Spain, and the vapours of the Holy League, began to disperse and threaten her felicity. Moreover, she was then to provide for some intestine strangers, which began to gather in the heart of her kingdom; all which had relation and correspondency, each one to the other, to dethrone her, and to disturb the public tranquillity, and therewithal, as a principal mark, the established religion, for the name of Recusant then began first to be known to the world; until then the Catholicks were no more than Church-Papists*, but now commanded by the pope's

* Because notwithstanding many dissented from the reformed establishment in many points of doctrine, and still acknowledged the pope's infallibility and supremacy; yet they looked not upon these doctrines and discipline to be fundamentals, or without which they could not be saved; and therefore continued to assemble and baptize, and communicate, for the space of ten years, in the Re-

exprefs Catholick Church, their mother, they separate themselves; so it seems the pope had then his aims to take a true number of his children; but the queen had the greater advantage, for she likewise took tale of her oppofite fubjects, their ftrength and how many they were, that had given their names to Baal, who* then by the hands of fome of his profelytes fixed his bulls on the gates of St. Paul's, which difcharged her fubjects of all fidelity, and received faith; and fo under the vail of the next fucceffor, to replant the Catholick religion. So that the queen had then a new tafk and work in hand, that might well awake her beft providence, and required a mufter of new arms, as well as courtfhips and counfels; for the time then began to grow quick and active, fitter for ftronger motions than them of the carpet and meafure; and it will be a true note of her magnanimity, that she loved a foldier, and had a propenfion in her nature to regard, and always to grace them; which the Court, taking into their confideration, took it as an inviting to win honour, together with her majefty's favour, by expofing themfelves to the wars, efpecially when the queen and the affairs of the kingdom ftood in fome neceffity of the foldiers; for we have many inftances of the fallies of the nobility and gentry, yea and of the

formed Church of England. Query whether their feparation did not make them fchifmaticks?

* The Pope.

Court and her privy-favourites, that had any touch or tincture of Mars in their inclinations, to steal away without licenfe, and the queen's privity; which had like to coft fome of them dear, fo predominant were their thoughts and hopes of honour grown in them, as we may truly obferve in the expofition of fir Philip Sidney, my lord of Effex and Mountjoy, and divers others whofe abfence, and the manner of their eruptions, was very diftafteful unto her; whereof I can hereunto add a true and no impertinent ftory, and that of the laft: Mountjoy, who having twice or thrice ftole away into Britanny, where under fir John Norris he had then a company, without the queen's leave and privity; fhe fent a meffenger unto him, with a ftrict charge to the general, to fee him fent home.

When he came into the queen's prefence, fhe fell into a kind railing, demanding of him how he durft go over without her leave: 'Serve me fo (quoth fhe) once more, and I will lay you faft enough for running; you will never leave till you are knocked on the head, as that inconfiderate fellow Sidney was; you fhall go when I fend; in the mean time, fee that you lodge in the court (which was then at Whitehall) where you may follow your book, read, and difcourfe of the wars.' But to our purpofe: It fell out happily to thofe, and, as I may fay, to thefe times, that the queen, during the calm time of her reign, was not idle, nor rocked afleep with fecurity; for fhe had been very provident in the reparation and augmentation of her shipping and ammunition, and I know not whether by a foresight of policy, or any instinct, it came about, or whether it was an act of her compassion; but it is most certain she sent no small troops to the revolted States of Holland, before she had received any affront from the king of Spain, that might deserve to tend to a breach of hostility, which the Papists maintain, to this day, was the provocation to the after wars; but, omitting what might be said to this point, these Netherland wars were the queen's seminaries, or nursery, of very many brave soldiers; and so likewise were the civil wars of France, whither she sent five several armies.

They were the French scholars that inured the youth and gentry of the kingdom, and it was a militia, where they were daily in acquaintance with the discipline of the Spaniards, who were then turned the queen's inveterate enemies.

And thus have I taken in observation her *dies Halcyonii*, i. e. these years of hers, which were more serene and quiet than those that followed, which though they were not less propitious, as being touched more with the points of honour and victory, yet were they troubled and loaded ever, both with domestick and foreign machinations; and as it is already quoted, they were such as awakened her spirits, and made her cast about her to defend, rather by offending, and by way of provision, to prevent all invasions, than to expect them; which was a

The Right Honble
SIR PHILIP SYDNEY, KNT.
From a Curious Limning by Oliver.
Published by E. Jeffery Pall Mall.

piece of the cunning of the times, and with this I have noted the causes and *principium* * of the wars following, and likewise points to the seed-plots, from whence she took up these brave men, and plants of honour, who acted on the theatre of Mars, and on whom she disperfed the rays of her graces; who were persons, in their kinds of care, virtuous, and such as might, out of their merit, pretend interest to her favours; of which rank the number will equal, if not exceed that of her gown men, in recount of whom I will proceed with sir Philip Sidney.

Sir PHILIP SIDNEY.

HE was the son of sir Henry Sidney, Lord Deputy of Ireland, and President of Wales, a person of great parts, and of no mean grace with the queen; his mother was sister to my lord of Leicester, from whence we may conjecture how the father stood up in the sphere of honour and employments, so that his descent was apparently noble on both sides; and, for his education, it was such as travel, and the University, could afford none better, and his tutors infuse; for, after an incredible proficiency in all the spheres of learning, he left the academical, for that of the Court, whither he came by his uncle's invitation, famed after by noble reports of his accomplishments, which together with the state of his person,

---

* Beginning.

framed by a natural propenfion to arms, foon attracted the good opinions of all men, and was fo highly praifed in the efteem of the queen, that fhe thought the Court deficient without him : and whereas, through the fame of his defert, he was in election for the kingdom of Pole *, fhe refufed to further his preferment : it was not out of emulation of advancement, but out of fear to lofe the jewel of her time. He married the daughter and fole heir of fir Francis Walfingham, the Secretary of State ; a lady deftinated to the bed of honour, who, after his deplorable death at Zutphen, in the Low Countries, where he was at the time of his uncle Leicefter's being there, was remarried to the lord of Effex, and, fince his death, to my lord of St. Albans, all perfons of the fword, and otherwife of great honour and virtue.

They have a very quaint conceit of him, that Mars and Mercury fell at variance, whofe fervant he fhould be; and there is an epigrammift that faith, that Art and Nature had fpent their excellencies in his fafhioning, and, fearing they could not end what they had begun, they beftowed him up for time, and Nature ftood mute, and amazed, to behold her own mark : but thefe are the particulars of poets.

Certain it is, he was a noble and matchlefs gentleman ; and it may be faid juftly of him, without

* Poland.

these hyperboles of faction, as it was of *Cato Uticensis*, That he seemed to be born only to that which he went about, *vir fatilis ingenii*, as Plutarch saith it; but to speak more of him were to make them less.

WALSINGHAM.

SIR Francis Walsingham, as we have said, had the honour to be sir Philip Sidney's father-in-law; he was a gentleman at first, of a good house, and of a better education, and from the University travelled for the rest of his learning; doubtless, he was the only linguist of his times, how to use his own tongue, whereby he came to be employed in the chiefest affairs of State.

He was sent ambassador to France, and staid there *Legar* long in the heat of the civil wars, and at the same time that Monsieur was here a suitor to the queen; and, if I be not mistaken, he played the very same part there, as since Gundamore did here*: at his return, he was taken principal Secretary, and for one of the great Engines of State, and of the times, high in his mistress the queen's favour, and a watchful servant over the safety of his mistress.

They note him to have certain courtesies and secret

* Gundamore, the Spanish ambassador, amused king James I. with much dissimulation.

ways of intelligence above the rest; but I must confess, I am to seek wherefore he suffered Parry * to play so long as he did, hang on the hook, before he hoised him up; and I have been a little curious in the search thereof, though I have not to do with the *Arcana Regalia Imperii*, for to know it is sometimes a burthen; and I remember it was Ovid's criminant error, that he saw too much, but I hope these are collaterals, and of no danger.

But that Parry, having an intent to kill the queen, made the way of his access, by betraying of others, and in impeaching of the priests of his own correspondency, and thereby had access to confer with the queen, as oftentimes private and familiar discourse with Walsingham, will not be the query of the mystery; for the secretary might have had an end of a further discovery and maturity of the treason; but that, after the queen knew Parry's intent, why she would then admit him to private discourse, and Walsingham to suffer him, considering the conditions of all the designs, and to permit him to go where and whither he listed, and only under the secrecy of a dark sentinel set over him, was a piece of reach and hazard, beyond my apprehension: I must again profess, that I have read many of his letters, for they are commonly sent to my lord of Leicester, and of Burleigh, out of France, containing many fine passages, and secrets, yet, if I might have been behold-

---

* The traytor, of whom hereafter in this collection.

ing to his cyphers, they would have told pretty tales of the times; but I muft now clofe him up, and rank him amongft the *Togati:* yet chief of thofe that laid the foundations of the French and Dutch wars, which was another piece of his finenefs of the times, with one obfervation more, that he was one of the greateft always of the Auftrian embracements, for both himfelf, and Stafford that preceded him, might well have been compared to him, in the Gofpel, that fowed his tares in the night ; fo did they their feeds in divifion, in the dark ; and as it is a likely report, that they father on him at his return, the queen fpeaking to him with fome fenfibility of the Spanifh defigns on France : madam, he anfwered, I befeech you be content, and fear not ; the Spaniard hath a great appetite and an excellent digeftion, but I have fitted him with a bone for thefe twenty years, that your majefty fhould have no caufe to doubt him, provided that, if the fire chance to fhake, which I have kindled, you will be ruled by me, and caft in fome of your fewel, which will revive the flame.

WILLOUGHBY.

MY lord Willoughby was one of the queen's firft fwords-men ; he was of the antient extract of the Bartewes, but more ennobled by his mother, who was duchefs of Suffolk ; he was a great mafter of the art *military,* and was fent general into France, and commanded the second army of five, the queen had sent thither, in aid of the French: I have heard it spoken, that, had he not slighted the court, but applied himself to the queen, he might have enjoyed a plentiful portion of her grace; and it was his saying, and it did him no good, that he was none of the *reptilia*, intimating that he could not creep on the ground, and that the court was not his element; for indeed, as he was a great soldier, so he was of a suitable magnanimity, and could not brook the obsequiousness and assiduity of the court; and as he was then somewhat descending from youth, happily he had an *animam revertendi*, or a desire to make a safe retreat.

BACON.

AND now I come to another of the *Togati*, sir Nicholas Bacon, an arch-piece of wit, and of wisdom; he was a gentleman, and a man of law, and of a great knowledge therein, whereby, together with his after-part of learning and dexterity, he was promoted to be keeper of the great Seal, and being of kin to the treasurer Burleigh, and * also the help of his hand to bring him to the queen's great favour, for he was abundantly factious; which took much with the queen, when it suited with the season, as he was well able to judge of the times: he had a very quaint saying, and he used it often to good

* *al.* Had.

purpose, *that he loved the jest well, but not the loss of his friend;* and that, though he knew that *verus quisque suæ fortunæ faber*, was a true and a good principle, yet the most in number were those that numbered themselves, but I will never forgive that man that loseth himself to be rid of his jests.

He was father to that refined wit, which since hath acted a disastrous part on the public stage, and of late sat in his father's room, as lord chancellor; those that lived in his age, and from whence I have taken this little model of him, give him a lively character, and they decipher him to be another *Solon*, and the *Simon* of those times, such a one as *Oedipus* was in dissolving of riddles; doubtless, he was an able instrument, as it was his commendation, that his head was the mallet, for it was a very great one, and therein kept a wedge, that entered all knotty pieces that came to the table.

And now again I must fall back to smooth and plain a way to the rest that is behind, but not from my purpose. There have been, about this time, two rivals in the queen's favour, old sir Francis Knowles, comptroller of the house, and sir Henry Norris, whom she had called up at parliament, to sit with the peers in the higher house; as, Henry Norris of Rycot, who had married the daughter and heir of the old Henry Williams of Tayne, a noble person, and to whom, in her adversity, the queen had been committed to his safe custody, and, from him, had received more than ordinary obfervances: now, fuch was the goodnefs of the queen's nature, that fhe neither forgot the good turns received from the lord Williams, neither was fhe unmindful of this lord Norris, whofe father, in her father's time, and in the bufinefs of her brother, died in a noble caufe, and in the juftification of her innocency.

NORRIS.

MY lord Norris had, by this lady, an apt iffue, which the queen highly refpected, for he had fix fons, and all martial and brave men: the firft was William the eldeft, and father to the late earl of Berkfhire; fir John, vulgarly called general Norris; fir Edward, fir Thomas, fir Henry, and Maximilian, men of haughty courage, and of great experience in the conduct of military affairs; and, to fpeak in the character of their merit, they were perfons of fuch renown and worth, as future times muft, of duty, owe them the debt of an honourable memory.

KNOWLES.

SIR Francis Knowles was fomewhat near in the queen's affinity, and had likewife no incompetent iffue; for he had alfo William, his eldeft fon, and fince earl of Banbury; fir Thomas, fir Robert, and fir Francis, if I be not a little miftaken in their names and marshaling: and there was also the lady Lettice, a sister of those, who was first countess of Essex, and after of Leicester; and those were also brave men in their times and places; but they were of the court and carpet, and not by the genius of the camp.

Between these two families there was, as it falleth out amongst great ones and competitors of favour, no great correspondency; and there were some seeds, either of emulation or distrust, cast between them; which had they not been disjoined in the residence of their persons, as that was the fortune of their employments, the one side attending the court, and the other the pavilion, surely they would have broken out into some kind of hostility, or, at least, they would intwine and wrestle one in the other, like trees circled with ivy; for there was a time, when, both these fraternities being met at court, there passed a challenge between them at certain exercises, the queen and the old men being spectators, which ended in a flat quarrel amongst them all: for I am persuaded, though I ought not to judge, that there were some relicks of this feigned, that were long after the causes of the one family's almost utter extirpation, and the other's inprosperity: for it was a known truth, that, so long as my lord of Leicester lived, who was the main pillar, on the one side, for having married the sister, the other side took no deep root in the court, though, otherwise, they made their ways to honour by their swords. And that, which is of more note, confidering my lord of Leicefter's ufe of men of war, being fhortly after fent governor to the revolted States, and no foldier himfelf, is, that he made no more account of fir John Norris, a foldier, then defervedly famoufed, and trained from a page under the difcipline of the greateft captain in Chriftendom, the admiral *Caftillian*, and of command in the French and Dutch wars almoft twenty years. And it is of further obfervation, that my lord of Effex, after Leicefter's deceafe, though addicted to arms, and honoured by the general in the Portugal expedition, whether out of inftigation, as it hath been thought, or out of ambition and jealoufy, eclipfed by the fame and fplendor of this great commander, never loved him in fincerity.

Moreover, and certain it is, he not only crufhed, and upon all occafions quelled the youth of this great man, and his famous brethren; but therewith drew on his own fatal end, by undertaking the Irifh action in a time when he left the court empty of friends, and full-fraught with his profeffed enemies. But I forbear to extend myfelf in any further relation upon this fubject, as having loft fome notes of truth in thefe two nobles, which I would prefent; and therewith touched fomewhat, which I would not, if the equity of the narration would have permitted any omiffion.

PERROT.

SIR John Perrot was a goodly gentleman, and of the fword; and he was of a very antient defcent, as an heir to many fubtracts of gentry, efpecially from Guy de Brian of Lawhorn; fo was he of a very vaft eftate, and came not to court for want, and to thefe advancements: he had the endowments of carriage and height of fpirit, had he alighted on the alloy and temper of difcretion; the defect whereof, with a native freedom and boldnefs of fpeech, drew him on to a clouded fitting, and laid him open to the fpleen and advantage of his enemies, of whom fir Chriftopher Hatton was profeffed; he was yet a wife man and a brave courtier, but rough, and participating more of active, than fedentary motions, as being in his inftillation deftined for arms. There is a query of fome denotations, how he came to receive the foil, and that in the cataftrophe? for he was ftrengthened with honourable alliances and the prime friendfhip in court, my lords of Leicefter and Burleigh, both his contemporaries and familiars; but that there might be (as the adage hath it) falfity in friendfhip: and we may reft fatisfied, that there is no difpute againft fate, and they quit him for a perfon that loved to ftand too much alone on his legs, of too often regrefs and difcontinuance from the queen's prefence, a fault which is incompatible with the ways of court and favour. He was fent lord deputy into Ireland, as it was then apprehended, for a kind of haughtinefs and repugnancy in council; or, as others have thought, the fitteft perfon, then, to bridle the infolencies of the Irifh; and probable it is, that both, confidering the fway that he would have at the board, being head in the queen's favour, concurred, and did alike confpire his remove and ruin: but into Ireland he went; where he did the queen very great and many fervices, if the furplufage of the meafure did not abate the value of the merit, as after-time found to be no paradox to fave the queen's purfe, but both herfelf, and my lord treafurer Burleigh, ever took for good fervice; he impofed on the Irifh the charge for bearing their own arms, which both gave them the poffeffion, and taught them the ufe of weapons; which provided, in the end, to a moft fatal work, both in the profufion of blood and treafure.

But, at his return, and upon fome account fent home before, touching the eftate of that kingdom, the queen poured out affiduous teftimonies of her grace towards him, till, by his retreat to his caftle of Cary, which he was then building, and out of a defire to be in command at home, as he had been abroad, together with the hatred and practice of Hatton, then in high favour, whom he had, not long before, bitterly taunted for his dancing, he was accufed for high treafon, and for high words, and a forged letter, and condemned; though the queen, on the news of his condemnation, fwore, by her wonted oath, that the jury were all knaves: and they delivered it with affurance, that, on his return to the town, after his trial, he faid, with oaths and with fury, to the lieutenant, fir Owen Hopton, What, will the queen fuffer her brother to be offered up as a facrifice to the envy of my flattering adverfaries? Which being made known to the queen, and fomewhat inforced, fhe refufed to fign it, and fwore he fhould not die, for he was an honeft and faithful man. And furely, though not altogether to fet our reft and faith upon tradition and old reports, as, That fir Thomas Perrot, his father, was a gentleman of the Privy-Chamber, and in the court married to a lady of great honour, which are prefumptions in fome implications; but, if we go a little further, and compare his pictures, his qualities, gefture, and voice, with that of the king, which memory retains yet amongft us, they will plead ftrongly, that he was a furreptitious child of the blood royal.

Certain it is, that he lived not long in the tower; and that, after his deceafe, fir Thomas Perrot, his fon, then of no mean efteem with the queen, having before married my lord of Effex's fifter, fince countefs of Northumberland, had reftitution of his land; though, after his death alfo (which immediately followed) the crown refumed the eftate, and took advantage of the former attainder; and, to fay the truth, the prieft's forged letter was, at his arraignment, thought but as a fiction of envy, and was, soon after, exploded by the priest's own confession: but that, which most exasperated the queen, and gave advantage to his enemies, was, as sir Walter Rawleigh takes into observation, words of disdain, for the queen, by sharp and reprehensive letters, had nettled him; and thereupon, sending others of approbation, commending his service, and intimating an invasion from Spain; which was no sooner proposed, but he said publickly, in the great chamber at Dublin: 'Lo, now she is ready to bepiss herself, for fear of the Spaniards; I am again one of her white boys:' which are subject to a various construction, and tended to some disreputation of his sovereign, and such as may serve for instruction to persons in place of honour and command, to beware of the violences of Nature, and especially the exorbitance of the tongue. And so I conclude him with this double observation; the one, of the innocency of his intentions, exempt and clear from the guilt of treason and disloyalty, therefore of the greatness of his heart; for, at his arraignment, he was so little dejected with what might be alledged, that rather he grew troubled with choler, and, in a kind of exasperation, he despised his jury, though of the order of knighthood, and of the especial gentry, claiming the privilege of trial by the peers and baronage of the realm: so prevalent was that of his native genius and haughtiness of spirit, which accompanied him to his last, and till, without any diminution of change therein, it brake in pieces the cords of his magnanimity; for he died suddenly in the tower, and when it was thought the queen did intend his enlargement, with the restitution of his possessions, which were then very great, and comparable to most of the nobility.

HATTON.

SIR Christopher Hatton came to the court, as his opposite; sir John Perrot was wont to say, by the galliard, for he came thither as a private gentleman of the inns of court, in a masque; and, for his activity and person, which was tall and proportionable, taken into her favour: he was first made Vice-chamberlain, and, shortly after, advanced to the place of Lord Chancellor; a gentleman that, besides the graces of his person, and dancing, had also the endowment of a strong and subtle capacity, and that could soon learn the discipline and garb, both of the times and court: and the truth is, he had a large proportion of gifts and endowments, but too much of the season of envy; and he was a mere vegetable of the court, that sprung up at night, and sunk again at his noon.

Flos non mentorum, sed sex fuit illa virorum.

EFFINGHAM.

MY lord of Effingham, though a courtier betimes, yet I find not that the sunshine of his favour brake out upon him, until she took him into the ship, and made him High Admiral of England; for his extract, it might suffice, that he was the son of A. Howard, and of A. duke of Norfolk.

And, for his person, as goodly a gentleman as the times had any, if Nature had not been more intentive to compleat his person, than Fortune to make him rich; for, the times confidered, which were then active, and a long time after lucrative, he died not wealthy; yet the honefter man, though, it feems the queen's purpofe was to render the occafion of his advancement, and to make him capable of more honour; at his return from the Cadiz voyage and action, she conferred it upon him, creating him earl of Nottingham, to the great difcontent of his colleague, my lord of Effex, who then grew exceffive in the appetite of her favour, and the truth is fo exorbitant in the limitation of the fovereign afpect, that it much alienated the queen's grace from him, and drew others together with the admiral to a combination, and confpire his ruin; and though, as I have heard it from that party (I mean the old admiral's faction) that it lay not in his proper power to hurt my lord of Effex, yet he had more fellows, and fuch as were well fkilled in the fetting of the train: but I leave this to thofe of another age; it is out of doubt, that the admiral was a good, honeft, and brave man, and a faithful fervant to his miftrefs; and fuch a one, as the queen, out of her own princely judgement, knew to be a fit inftrument in her service, for she was a proficient in the reading of men, as well as books; and as sundry expeditions, as that aforementioned, and 88, do better express his worth, and manifest the queen's trust, and the opinion she had of his fidelity and conduct.

Moreover, the Howards were of the queen's alliance, and consanguinity, by her mother, which swayed her affections, and bent it towards this great house; and it was a part of her natural propension to grace and support antient nobility, where it did not intrench, neither invade her interest; from such trespasses she was quick and tender, and would not spare any whatsoever, as we may observe in the case of the duke, and my lord of Hertford, whom she much favoured, and countenanced, till they attempted the forbidden fruit, the fault of the last being, in the severest interpretation, but a trespass of incroachment; but in the first it was taken as a riot against the crown, and her own sovereign power, and as I have ever thought the cause of her aversion, against the rest of that house, and the duke's great father-in-law, Fitz-Allen, earl of Arundel, a person in the first rank of her affections, before these, and some other jealousies, made a separation between them.

This noble lord, and lord Thomas Howard, since earl of Suffolk, standing alone in her grace, and the rest in her umbrage.

PACKINGTON.

SIR John Packington was a gentleman of no mean family, and of form and feature no ways difabled, for he was a brave gentleman, and a very fine courtier, and for the time which he ftayed there, which was not lafting, very high in her grace; but he came in, and went out, through difaffiduity, drew the curtain between himfelf and the light of her grace, and then death overwhelmed the remnant, and utterly deprived him of recovery; and they fay of him, that, had he brought lefs to her court than he did, he might have carried away more than he brought, for he had a time on it, but was an ill hufband of opportunity.

HUNSDOWN.

MY lord of Hunfdown was of the queen's nearest kindred, and, on the deceafe of Suffex, both he and his fon fucceffively took the place of Lord Chamberlain; he was a man faft to his prince, and firm to his friends and fervants; and though he might fpeak big, and therein would be borne out, yet was he the more dreadful, but lefs harmful, and far from the practice of the lord of Leicefter's inftructions, for he was downright; and I have heard thofe that both knew him well, and had intereft in him, fay merrily of him, that his Latin and diffimulation were alike; and that his cuftom of fwearing and obfcenity, in fpeaking, made him feem a worfe Chriftian than he was, and a better knight of her carpet than he could be. As he lived in a roughling time, fo he loved fword and buckler-men, and fuch as our fathers were wont to call men of their hands; of which fort he had many brave gentlemen that followed him, yet not taken for a popular and dangerous perfon: and this is one that ftood among the *Togati*, of an honeft, ftout heart, and fuch a one, that, upon occafion, would have fought for his prince and country, for he had the charge of the queen's perfon, both in the court and in the camp at Tilbury.

RAWLEIGH.

SIR Walter Rawleigh was one that, it feems, Fortune had picked out of purpofe, of whom to make an example, and to ufe as her tennis-ball, thereby to fhew what fhe could do, for fhe toffed him up of nothing, and to and fro to greatnefs, and from thence down to little more than to that wherein fhe found him, a bare gentleman; and not that he was lefs, for he was well defcended, and of good alliance, but poor in his beginnings: and for my lord Oxford's jefts of him for the jacks and upftarts, we all know it favoured more of emulation, and his honour, than of truth; and it is a certain note of the times, that the queen, in her choice, never took in her favour a mere viewed man, or a mechanick, as Comines obferves of Lewis XI. who did ferve himfelf with perfons of unknown parents, fuch as were Oliver the barber, whom he created earl of Dunoyes, and made him *ex fecretis confiliis*, and alone in his favour and familiarity.

His approaches to the Univerfity and inns of court were the grounds of his improvement, but they were rather extrufions than fieges, or fettings down, for he ftaid not long in a place; and, being the youngeft brother, and the houfe diminifhed in his patrimony, he forefaw his deftiny, that he was firft to roll through want and difability, to fubfift otherwife, before he came to a repofe, and as the ftone doth by long lying gather mofs. He was the firft that expofed himfelf in the land-fervice of Ireland, a militia which did not then yield him food and raiment, for it was ever very poor; nor dared he to ftay long there, though fhortly after he came thither again, under the command of the lord Grey, but with his own colours flying in the field, having, in the interim, caft a mere chance, both in the Low Countries, and in the voyage to fea; and, if ever man drew virtue out of neceffity, it was he, and therewith was he the great example of induftry; and though he might then have taken that of the merchant to himfelf,

Per mare, per terras, currit mercator ad Indos,

He might alfo have faid, and truly, with the philo-
fopher, *Omnia mea mecum porto*, for it was a long
time before he could brag of more than he carried at
his back ; and when he got on the winning fide, it
was his commendation, that he took pains for it,
and underwent many various adventures for his
after-perfection, and before he came into the publick note of the world ; and thence may appear how
he came up *per ardua ;*

Per varios cafus, per tot difcrimina rerum,

Not pulled up by chance, nor by any great admit-
tance ; I will only defcribe his natural parts, and
thefe of his own acquiring.

He had, in the outward man, a good prefence,
in a handfome and well-compacted perfon ; a ftrong
natural wit, and a better judgement, with a bold
and plaufible tongue, whereby he could fet out his
parts to the beft advantage ; and thefe he had by the
adjuncts of fome general learning, which by dili-
gence he enforced to a great augmentation and perfection, for he was an indefatigable reader, by fea
and land, and one of the beft obfervers, both of
men, and of the times ; and I am fomewhat confident, that, among the fecond caufes of his growth,
there was variance between him and my lord general Grey, in his fecond defcent into Ireland, which
drew them both over to the council-table, there to
plead their own caufes ; where what advantage he

had in the cafe in controverfy, I know not, but he had much the better in the manner of telling his tale, infomuch as the queen and the lords took no flight mark of the man, and his parts; for from thence he came to be known, and to have accefs to the lords; and then we are not to doubt how fuch a man would comply to progeffion; and whether or no my lord of Leicefter had then caft a good word for him to the queen, which would have done him no harm, I do not determine; but true it is, he had gotten the queen's ear in a trice, and fhe began to be taken with his election, and loved to hear his reafons to her demands: and, the truth is, fhe took him for a kind of oracle, which nettled them all; yea, thofe that he relied on, began to take this his fudden favour for an alarm, and to be fenfible of their own fupplantation, and to project his, which made him fhortly after fing,

Fortune, my foe, why doft thou frown?

So that, finding his favour declining, and falling into a recefs, he undertook a new peregrination, to leave that *terra infirma* *, of the court, for that of the waves, and by declining himfelf, and by abfence, to expel his, and the paffion of his enemies; which, in court, was a ftrange device of recovery, but that he then knew there was fome ill office done him; yet he durft not attempt to mend it, otherwife

* Inftability.

than by going afide thereby, to teach envy a new way of forgetfulnefs, and not fo much as think of him. Howfoever, he had it always in mind, never to forget himfelf; and his device took fo well, that in his return he came in as rams do, by going backward with the greater ftrength, and fo continued to the laft, great in her favour, and captain of her guard: where I muft leave him, but with this obfervation, though he gained much at the court, he took it not out of the exchequer, or merely out of the queen's purfe, but by his wit, and by the help of the prerogative; for the queen was never profufe in delivering out of her treafure, but paid moft and many of her fervants, part in money, and the reft with grace; which, as the cafe ftood, was then taken for good payment, leaving the arrears of recompence due for their merit, to her great fucceffor [*], who paid them all with advantage [†].

GREVILLE.

SIR Foulke Greville, fince lord Brooke, had no mean place in her favour, neither did he hold it for any fhort time, or term; for, if I be not deceived, he had the longeft leafe, the fmootheft time, with-

---

[*] James the Firft.

[†] He, difhonourably, cut off this good fervant's head, and feized upon his eftate.

out rubs of any of her favourites; he came to the court in his youth and prime, as that is the time, or never; he was a brave gentleman, and hopefully defcended from Willoughby, lord Brooke, and admiral to Henry the feventh; neither illiterate, for he was, as he would often profefs, a friend to fir Philip Sidney, and there are now extant fome fragments of his pen, and of the times, which do intereft him in the Mufes, and which fhew in him the queen's election had ever a noble conduct, and it motions more of virtue and judgement, than of fancy.

I find, that he neither fought for, nor obtained any great place, or preferment in court, during all his time of attendance; neither did he need it, for he came thither backed with a plentiful fortune, which, as himfelf was wont to fay, was then better held together by a fingle life, wherein he lived, and died a conftant courtier of the ladies.

ESSEX.

MY lord of Effex, as fir Henry Walton notes him, a gentleman of great parts, and partly of his times, and retinue, had his introduction by my lord of Leicefter, who had married his mother; a tie of affinity, which, befides a more urgent obligation, might have invited his care to advance him, his fortunes being then, through his father's infelicity, grown low; but that the son of a lord Ferrers of Chartly, vifcount Hertford, and earl of Effex, who was of the antient nobility, and formerly in the queen's good grace, could not have room in her favour, without the affiftance of Leicefter, was beyond the rule of her nature, which, as I have elfewhere taken into obfervation, was ever inclinable to favour the nobility: fure it is, that he no fooner appeared in court, but he took with the queen and the courtiers; and, I believe, they all could not chufe but look through the facrifice of the father on his living fon, whofe image, by the remembrance of former paffages, was a frefh leek, the bleeding of men murdered, reprefented to the court, and offered up as a fubject of compaffion to all the kingdom.

There was in this young lord, together with a goodly perfon, a kind of urbanity and innate courtefy, which both won the queen, and too much took up the people to gaze on the new-adopted fon of her favour; and as I go along, it will not be amifs to take into obfervation two notable quotations; the firft was a violent indulgence of the queen (which is incident to old age, where it encounters with a pleafing and fuitable object) towards this great lord, which argued a non-perpetuity; the fecond was a fault in the object of her grace, my lord himfelf, who drew in too faft, like a child fucking on an over uberous nurfe; and had there been a more decent decorum obferved in both, or either of thefe, without doubt, the unity of their affections had been more permanent, and not so in and out, as they were, like an instrument well tuned, and lapsing to discord.

The greater error of the two, though unwilling, I am constrained to impose on my lord of Essex, and rather on his youth, and none of the least of the blame on those that stood sentinels about him, who might have advised better, but that like men, intoxicated with hopes, they likewise had sucked in with the most of their lord's receipts, and so, like Cæsars, would have all or none; a rule quite contrary to Nature, and the most indulgent parents, who, though they may express more affection to one in the abundance of bequeaths, yet cannot forget some legacies, and distributives, and dividends to others of their begetting; and how hurtful partiality is, and proves, every day's experience tells us, out of which common consideration, they might have framed to their hands a maxim of more discretion, for the conduct and management of their new-graved lord and master.

But to omit that of infusion, and to do right to truth, my lord of Essex, even of those that truly loved and honoured him, was noted for too bold an ingrosser, both of fame and favour; and of this, without offence to the living, or treading on the sacred grave of the dead, I shall present the truth of a passage, yet in memory.

My lord of Mountjoy, who was another child of her favour, being newly come, and then but fir Charles Blount (for my lord William, his elder brother, was then living) had the good fortune to run one day well at Tilt, and the queen was therewith fo well pleafed, that fhe fent him, in token of her favour, a queen at chefs in gold, richly enamelled, which his fervants had, the next day, faftened unto his arm, with a crimfon ribband; which my lord of Effex, as he paffed through the Privy Chamber, efpying with his cloak caft under his arm, the better to command it to the view, enquired what it was, and for what caufe there fixed: fir Foulke Greville told him, it was the queen's favour, which the day before, and next after the tilting, fhe had fent him; whereat my lord of Effex, in a kind of emulation, and as though he would have limited her favour, faid, Now I perceive, every fool muft have a favour. This bitter and publick affront came to fir Charles Blount's ear, at which he fent him a challenge; which was accepted by my lord, and they met near Marybone Park, where my lord was hurt in the thigh, and difarmed; the queen, miffing of the men, was very curious to learn the truth, but at laft it was whifpered out; fhe fware by God's Death, it was fit that fome one or other fhould take him down, and teach him better manners, otherwife there would be no rule with him; and here I note the imminution of my lord's friendfhip with Mountjoy, which the queen herfelf did then conjure.

Now for his fame we need not go far, for my lord of Essex, having borne a grudge to general Norris, who had unwittingly offered to undertake the action of Britanny, with fewer men than my lord had before demanded; on his return with victory, and a glorious report of his valour, he was then thought the only man for the Irish wars; wherein my lord of Essex so wrought, by despising the number and quality of the rebels, that Norris was sent over with a scanty force, joined with the relicks of the veteran troops of Britain, of set purpose, and as it fell out, to ruin Norris; and the lord Burrows, by my lord's procurement, sent at his heels, and to command in chief, and to convey Norris only to his government at Munster; which aggravated the great heart of the general, to see himself undervalued, and undermined, by my lord and Burrows, which was, as the Proverb speaks, *juvenes docere senes*.

Now my lord Burrows in the beginning of his prosecution died, whereupon the queen was fully bent to send over my lord Mountjoy; which my lord of Essex utterly misliked, and opposed with many reasons, and by arguments of contempt towards Mountjoy (his then professed friend and familiar) so predominant was his desire to reap the whole honour of closing up that war, and all others; now the way being paved, and opened, by his own workmanship, and so handled, that none durst appear to stand in the place; at last, and with much ado, he obtained his own ends, and therewith his fatal destruction, leaving the queen and the court, where he stood impregnable and firm in her grace, to men that long had sought and waited their times to give him a trip, and could never find any opportunity, but this of his abfence, and of his own creation; and thofe are true obfervations of his appetite and inclinations, which were not of any true proportion, but hurried, and tranfported, with an over defire, and thirftinefs after fame, and that deceitful fame of popularity; and, to help on his cataftrophe, I obferve likewife two forts of people, that had a hand in his fall: The firft was the foldiery, which all flock unto him, as it were foretelling a mortality, and are commonly of blunt and too rough counfels, and many times diffonant from the time of the court and State; the other fort were of his family, his fervants and his own creatures, fuch as were bound by fafety, and obligations of fidelity, to have looked better to the fteering of that boat, wherein they themfelves were carried, and not to have fuffered it to fleet, and run on ground, with thofe empty fails of tumor of popularity and applaufe; methinks one honeft man or other, who had but the brufhing of his cloaths, might have whifpered in his ear, my lord, look to it, this multitude, that follows you, will either devour you, or undo you; do not ftrive to over-rule all, for it will coft hot water, and it will procure envy, and if needs your genius muft have it fo, let the court and the queen's prefence be your ftation, for your abfence muft undo you. But, as I have faid, they had fucked too much of their

lord's milk, and inſtead of withdrawing they drew *
the coals of his ambition, and infuſed into him too
much of the ſpirit of glory, yea, and mixed the good-
neſs of his nature, with a touch of revenge, which
is evermore accompanied with a deſtiny of the ſame
fate. Of this number, there were ſome of inſuffer-
able natures about him, that towards his laſt gave
deſperate advice, ſuch as his integrity abhorred, and
his fidelity forbade, amongſt whom ſir Henry Walton
notes, without injury, his ſecretary Cuffe, as a vile
man, and of a perverſe nature: I could alſo name
others, that, when he was in the right courſe of recovery, ſettling to moderation, would not ſuffer a
receſs in him, but ſtirred up the dregs of thoſe rude
humours, which, by times and his affections out of
his own judgement, he thought to repoſe, and give
them a vomit. And thus I conclude this noble lord,
as a mixture between proſperity and adverſity, once
a child of his great miſtreſs's favour, but a ſon of
Bellona.

BUCKHURST.

MY lord of Buckhurſt was of the noble houſe of
Sackvilles, and of the queen's conſanguinity, or as
the people then called him *Fill-ſacks*, by reaſon of
his great wealth, and the vaſt patrimony left to his
ſon, whereof in his youth he ſpent the beſt part, until the queen, by her frequent admonitions, diverted

* *al.* Blew

the torrent of his profusion; he was a very fine gentleman, of person and endowments, both of art and nature, but without measure magnificent, till on the turn of his honour, and the alloy, that his yearly good counsel had wrought upon those immoderate courses of his youth, and that height of spirit inherent to his house; and then did the queen, as a most judicious, indulgent prince, who, when she saw the man grown settled and staid, gave him an assistance, and advanced him to the treasurership, where he made amends to his house, for his mis-spent time, both in the increasement of his estate and honour, which the queen conferred upon him, together with the opportunity to remake himself, and thereby to shew that this was a child, that should have a share in her grace.

They much commend his elocution, but more the excellency of his pen, for he was a scholar, and a person of a quick dispatch, faculties that yet run in the blood; and they say of him, that his secretaries did little for him, by the way of indictment, wherein they could seldom please him, he was so facete and choice in his phrases and stile; and for his dispatches, and for the content he gave to suitors, he had a decorum seldom put in practice, for he had of his attendance that took into a roll the names of all suitors, with the date of their first addresses; so that a fresh man could not leap over his head, that was of a more antient edition, excepting the urgent affairs of the State.

I find not, that he was any way enfnared in the factions of the court, which were all his times ftrong, and in every man's note, the Howards and the Cecills of the one part, and my lord of Effex, &c. on the other, for he held the ftaff of the treafury faft in his hand, which made them, once in a year, to be beholden to him; and the truth is, as he was a wife man, and a ftout, he had no reafon to be a partaker, for he ftood fure in blood and in grace, and was wholly intentive to the queen's fervice; and fuch were his abilities, that fhe might have more cunning inftruments, but none of a more ftrong judgement, and confidence in his ways, which are fymptoms of magnanimity, whereunto methinks this motto hath fome kind of reference, *Aut nunquam tentes, aut perfice*. As though he would have charactered, in a word, the genius of his houfe, or exprefs fomewhat of a higher inclination, than lay within his compafs; that he was a courtier is apparent, for he ftood always in her eye, and in her favour.

MOUNTJOY.

MY lord Mountjoy was of the antient nobility, but utterly decayed in the fupport thereof, patrimony, through his grandfather's excefs, his father's vanity in fearch of the Philofophers-ftone, and his brother's untimely prodigality; all which feemed, by a joint confpiracy, to ruinate the houfe, and altogether to annihilate it; as he came from Oxford, he took the inner temple in the way to court, whither he no sooner came, but he had a pretty kind of admission, which I have heard from a discreet man of his own, and much more of the secrets of those times; he was then much about twenty years of age, brown-haired, of a sweet face, and of a most neat composure, tall in his person; the queen was then at White-hall, and at dinner, whither he came to see the fashion of the court, and the queen had soon found him out, and, with a kind of an affected favour, asked her carver who he was; he answered he knew him not, insomuch that an inquiry was made, one from another, who he might be, till at length it was told the queen, he was brother to the lord William Mountjoy. Thus inquiry, with the eye of her majesty fixed upon him, as she was wont to do, and to daunt men she knew not, stirred the blood of the young gentleman, insomuch as his colour went and came; which the queen observing, called unto him, and gave him her hand to kiss, encouraging him with gracious words, and new looks, and so diverting her speech to the lords, and ladies, she said, that she no sooner observed him, but she knew there was in him some noble blood, with some other expressions of pity towards his house; and then, again demanding his name, she said, fail you not to come to the court, and I will bethink myself, how to do you good; and this was his inlet, and the beginning of his grace; where it falls into consideration, that, though he wanted not wit, nor courage, for he had very fine attractives, as being a good piece of a scholar, yet were thofe accompanied with the retractives of bafhfulnefs, and natural modefty, which, as the wave of the houfe of his fortune then ftood, might have hindered his progreffion, had they not been reinforced by the infufion of fovereign favour, and the queen's gracious invitation; and that it may appear how he was, and how much that heretick, neceffity, will work in the directions of good fpirits, I can deliver it with affurance, that his exhibition was very fcanty, untill his brother died, which was fhortly after his admiffion to the court; and then was it no more but a thoufand marks *per annum*, wherewith he lived plentifully, and in a fine garb, and without any great fuftentation of the queen, during all her times.

And, as there was in nature a kind of backwardnefs, which did not befriend him, nor fuit with the motion of the court, fo there was in him an inclination to arms, with an humour of travelling, and gadding abroad, which had not fome wife men about him laboured to remove, and the queen laid in her command, he would, out of his own native propenfion, marred his own market; for as he was grown by reading, whereunto he was much addicted, to the theory of a foldier, fo was he ftrongly invited by his genius, to the acquaintance of the practice of the war, which were the caufes of his excurfions, for he had a company in the Low Countries,

from whom he came over with a noble acceptance
of the queen; but, somewhat restless in honourable
thoughts, he exposed himself again and again, and
would press the queen with pretences of visiting his
company so often, till at length he had a flat denial;
yet he struck over with sir John Norris into the action
of Britanny, which was then a hot and active war,
whom he would always call his father, honouring
him above all men, and ever bewailing his end; so
contrary he was in his esteem and valuation of this
great commander, to that of his friend, my lord of
Essex; till at last the queen began to take his digres-
sions for contempt, and confined his residence to the
court *, and her own presence; and, upon my lord
of Essex's fall, so confident she was of her own
princely judgement, and the opinion she had con-
ceived of his worth and conduct, that she would have
this noble gentleman, and none other, to bring in
the Irish wars to a propitious end; for it was a pro-
phetical speech of her own, that it would be his fortune, and his honour, to cut the thread of that fatal
rebellion, and to bring her in peace to the grave;
wherein she was not deceived: for he achieved it,
but with much pains and carefulness, and not without the forces and many jealousies of the court and
times, wherewith the queen's age and the malignity
of her settling times were replete. And so I come
to his dear friend in court, secretary Cecill, whom,

* As related before, in the account of secretary William
Cecill.

in his long abfence, he adored as his faint, and counted him his only *Mecenas*, both before and after his departure from court, and during all the time of his command in Ireland; well knowing, that it lay in his power, and by a word of his mouth, to make or mar him.

ROBERT CECILL.

SIR Robert Cecill, fince earl of Salifbury, was the fon of the lord Burleigh, and, by degrees, fucceffor of his places and favours, though not of his lands; for he had fir Thomas Cecill his elder brother, fince created earl of Exeter; he was firft fecretary of State, then mafter of the Court of Wards, and, in the laft of her reign, came to be lord treafurer: all which were the fteps of his father's greatnefs, and of the honour he left to his houfe. For his perfon, he was not much beholden to Nature, though fomewhat for his face, which was the beft part of his outfide: for his infide, it may be faid, and without offence, that he was his father's own fon, and a pregnant precedent in all his difcipline of ftate: he was a courtier from his cradle, which might have made him betimes; but he was at the age of twenty, and upwards, and was far fhort of his after-proof, but expofed, and by change of climate, he foon made fhew, what he was, and would be.

Robert Cecil,
Earl of Salisbury.

He lived in thofe times, wherein the queen had moft need and ufe of men of weight; and, amongft many able ones, this was chief, as having taken his fufficiency from his inftruction who begat him, the tutorfhip of the times and court, which were then academies of Art and Cunning. For fuch was the queen's condition, from the tenth, or twelfth of her reign, that fhe had the happinefs to ftand up, whereof there is a former intimation, environed with many and more enemies, and affaulted with more dangerous practices, than any prince of her times, and of many ages before: where we muft not, in this her prefervation, attribute it to human power, for that, in his own omnipotent providence, God ordained thofe fecondary means, as inftruments of the work, by an evident manifeftation of the fame work, which fhe acted; and it was a well-pleafing work of his own, out of a peculiar care he had decreed the protection of the work-miftrefs, and, thereunto, added his abundant bleffing upon all and whatfoever fhe undertook: which is an obfervation of fatisfaction to myfelf, that fhe was in the right; though, to others now breathing under the fame form and frame of her government, it may not feem an animadverfion of their worth: but I leave them to the peril of their own folly, and fo come again to this great minifter of State and the ftaff of the queen's declining age; who, though his little, crooked perfon could not promife any great fupportation, yet it carried thereon a head, and a head-piece, of a vaft content; and therein, it feems, Nature was fo diligent to compleat one and the best part about him, as the perfection of his memory and intellectuals: she took care also of his senses, and to put him in *lynceos oculos*, or, to pleasure him the more, borrowed of Argos, so to give unto him a prospective sight; and, for the rest of his sensitive virtues, his predecessor, Walsingham, had left him a receipt to smell out what was done in the conclave.

And his good old father was so well seen in mathematicks, that he could tell you, throughout Spain, every part, every port, every ship, with its burden; whither bound, what preparations, what impediments for diversion of enterprises, counsel, and resolution; and, that we may see, as in a little map, how docible this little man was, I will present a taste of his abilities.

My lord of Devonshire, upon certainty that the Spaniards would invade Ireland with a strong army, had written very earnestly to the queen, and to the council, for such supplies to be timely sent over, that might enable him both to march up to the Spaniard, if he did land, and follow on his prosecution without diverting his intentions against the rebels. Sir Robert Cecill, besides the general dispatch of the council (as he often did) writ thus in private, for these two then began to love dearly:

"My lord, out of the abundance of my affection, and the care I have of your well-doing, I must in private put you out of doubt or fear, for I know you cannot be fenfible, otherwife than in the way of honour, that the Spaniards will not come unto you this year; for I have it from my own, what his preparations are in all his parts, and what he can do; for, be confident, he beareth up a reputation, by feeming to embrace more than he can gripe; but, the next year, be affured, he will caft over to you fome forlorn troops, which, how they may be reinforced beyond his prefent ability, and his firft intention, I cannot, as yet, make any certain judgement; but I believe, out of my intelligence, that you may expect the landing in Munfter, and, the more to diftract you, in feveral places, as, at Kinfale, Beerhaven, and Baltimore; where, you may be fure, coming from fea, they will firft fortify, and learn the ftrength of the rebels, before they dare take the field. Howfoever, as I know you will not leffen your care, neither your defences, whatfoever lies in my power to do you and the public fervice, reft thereof affured."

And to this I could add much more, but it may (as it is) fuffice to prefent much of his abilities in the pen, that he was his crafts-mafter in foreign intelligence, and for domeftick affairs. As he was one of thofe that fat at the helm to the laft of the queen, fo was he none of the leaft in fkill, and in the true ufe of the compafs; and fo I fhall only vindicate the fcandal of his death, and conclude him; for he departed at St. Margaret's, near Marlborough, at his return from Bath, as my lord vice-chamberlain, my lord Clifford, and myfelf his fon, and fon-in-law, and many more can witnefs: but that, the day before, he fwooned on the way, and was taken out of his litter, and laid into his coach, was a truth, out of which that falfehood, concerning the manner of his death, had its derivation, though nothing to the purpofe, or to the prejudice of his worth.

VERE.

SIR Francis Vere was of that antient, and of the moft noble extract of the earls of Oxford; and it may be a queftion whether the nobility of his houfe, or the honour of his achievments, might moft commend him, but that we have an authentick rule:

Nam genus & proavos & quæ nos non fecimus ipfi,
Vix ea noftra voco.———

For though he was an honourable flip of that antient tree of nobility, which was no difadvantage to his virtue, yet he brought more glory to the name of Vere, than he took of blood from the family.

He was, amongft all the queen's fwordfmen, inferior to none, but fuperior to many; of whom it may be faid, to fpeak much of him were the way to leave out fomewhat that might add to his praife, and to forget more than would make to his honour.

I find not that he came much to the court, for he lived almoft perpetually in the camp; but, when he died, no man had more of the queen's favour, and none lefs envied, for he feldom troubled it with the noife and alarms of fupplications; his way was another fort of undermining.

They report that the queen, as fhe loved martial men, would court this gentleman, as foon as he appeared in her prefence; and furely he was a foldier of great worth and command, thirty years in the fervice of the States, and twenty years over the Englifh in chief, as the queen's general: and he, that had feen the battle of Newport, might there beft have taken him and his noble brother *, the lord of Tilbury, to the life.

WORCESTER.

MY lord of Worcefter I have here put laft, but not leaft in the queen's favour; he was of the antient and noble blood of the Beauforts, and of her † grandfather's kin by the mother, which the queen could never forget, efpecially where there was an incurrence of old blood with fidelity, a mixture which ever forted with the queen's nature; and though there might hap fomewhat in this houfe, which might invert her grace, though not to fpeak

* Horatio.   † Elizabeth's.

of my lord himfelf but in due reverence and honour, I mean contrariety or fufpicion in religion; yet the queen ever refpected his houfe, and principally his noble blood, whom fhe firft made mafter of her horfe, and then admitted him of her council of ftate.

In his youth, part whereof he fpent before he came to refide at court, he was a very fine gentleman, and the beft horfeman and tilter of the times, which were then the manlike and noble recreations of the court, and fuch as took up the applaufe of men, as well as the praife and commendation of ladies; and when years had abated thofe exercifes of honour, he grew then to be a faithful and profound counfellor; and as I have placed him laft, fo was he the laft liver of all her fervants of her favour, and had the honour to fee his renowned miftrefs, and all of them, laid in the places of their refts; and for himfelf, after a life of very noble and remarkable reputation, and in a peaceable old age, a fate that I make the laft, and none of my flighteft obfervations, which befel not many of the reft, for they expired like unto a light blown out with the fnuff ftinking, not commendably extinguifhed, and with an offence to the ftanders-by. And thus I have delivered up my poor effay, or little draught of this great princefs and her times, with the fervants of her ftate and favour. I cannot fay I have finifhed it, for I know how defective and imperfect it is, as limbed only in the original nature, not without the active blessings, and so left it as a task fitter for remoter times, and the sallies of some bolder pencil to correct that which is amiss, and draw the rest up to life, than for me to have endeavoured it. I took it in consideration, how I might have dashed into it much of the stain of pollution, and thereby have defaced that little which is done; for I profess I have taken care to master my pen, that I might not err *animo**, or of set purpose discolour each or any of the parts thereof, otherwise than in concealment. Haply there are some who will not approve of this modesty, but will censure it for pusillanimity, and, with the cunning artist, attempt to draw their line further out at length, and upon this of mine, which way (with somewhat more ease) it may be effected; for that the frame is ready made to their hands, and then haply I could draw one in the midst of theirs, but that modesty in me forbids the defacements in men departed, their posterity yet remaining, enjoying the merit of their virtues, and do still live in their honour. And I had rather incur the censure of abruption, than to be conscious and taken in the manner, sinning by eruption, or trampling on the graves of persons at rest, which living we durst not look in the face, nor make our addresses unto them, otherwise than with due regard to their honours, and reverence to their virtues.

* Willingly.

LORD HERBERT.

THE accomplifhed, the brave, and romantick lord Herbert of Cherbury, was born in this reign, and laid the foundation of that admirable learning of which he was afterwards a complete mafter.

FINIS.

DIRECTIONS *for placing the* PLATES.

	PAGE
Queen Elizabeth before the Title	
Windfor Caftle	48
Cardinal Wolfey	51
Nonfuch	58
Earl of Southampton	66
Lord Howard	67
Lord Leicefter	97
Marquis of Winchefter	103
Sir Philip Sydney	109
Earl of Salifbury	144
Lord Herbert	152

Edward Lord Herbert of Cherbury.

*From the Miniature by Isaac Oliver, in the Possession of the R.t Hon.ble the Earl of Oxford.
Published as the Act directs May 1.1797 by E. Jeffery Pall Mall.*

www.ingramcontent.com/pod-product-compliance
Lightning Source LLC
Chambersburg PA
CBHW031446160426
43195CB00010BB/876